Margi

S E R I E S

A life-changing encounter
with God's Word from the books of

JEREMIAH &
LAMENTATIONS

D1113212

NAVPRESS

Discipleship Inside Out®

NAVPRESS
Discipleship Inside Out®

NavPress is the publishing ministry of The Navigators, an international Christian organization and leader in personal spiritual development. NavPress is committed to helping people grow spiritually and enjoy lives of meaning and hope through personal and group resources that are biblically rooted, culturally relevant, and highly practical.

For a free catalog go to www.NavPress.com
or call 1.800.366.7788 in the United States or 1.800.839.4769 in Canada.

ISBN-13: 978-1-61521-765-6

Printed in the United States of America

1 2 3 4 5 6 7 8 / 18 17 16 15 14 13

CONTENTS

HOW TO USE THIS STUDY

Although the LifeChange guides vary with the individual books they explore, they share some common goals:

1. To provide you with a firm foundation of understanding, plus a thirst to return to the books of Jeremiah and Lamentations throughout your life

2. To give you study patterns and skills that help you explore every part of the Bible

3. To offer you historical background, word definitions, and explanation notes to aid your study

4. To help you grasp as a whole the message of Jeremiah and Lamentations

5. To teach you how to let God's Word transform you into Christ's image

As You Begin

This guide includes twelve lessons that will take you chapter by chapter through Jeremiah and Lamentations. Each lesson is designed to take from one to two hours of preparation to complete on your own. To benefit most from this time, here's a good way to begin your work on each lesson:

1. Pray for God's help to keep you mentally alert and spiritually sensitive.

2. Read attentively through the entire passage mentioned in the lesson's title.

(You may want to read the passage from two or more Bible versions —perhaps at least once from a more literal translation such as the New International Version, English Standard Version, New American Standard Bible, or New King James Version, and perhaps once more in a paraphrase such as *The Message* or the New Living Translation.) Do your reading in an environment that's as free as possible from distractions. Allow your mind and heart to meditate on these words you encounter, words that are God's personal gift to you and to all His people.

After reading the passage, you're ready to dive into the numbered questions for the chapter, which make up the main portion of each lesson. Each of the questions is followed by blank space for writing your answers. This act of writing your answers helps clarify your thinking and stimulates your mental engagement with the passage, as well as your later recall. Use extra paper or a notebook if the space for recording your answers seems too cramped. Continue through the questions in numbered order. If any question seems too difficult or unclear, just skip it and go on to the next.

Most of the questions will direct you back to Jeremiah and Lamentations to look again at a certain portion of the assigned passage for that lesson. At that point be sure to use a more literal Bible translation, rather than a paraphrase.

As you look closer at the passage, it's helpful to approach it in this progression:

Observe. What does the passage actually *say*? Ask God to help you see it clearly. Notice everything that's there.

Interpret. What does the passage *mean*? Ask God to help you understand. And remember that any passage's meaning is fundamentally determined by its *context*. So stay alert to all you'll see about the setting and background of Jeremiah and Lamentations, and keep thinking of these books as a whole while you proceed through them chapter by chapter. You'll be progressively building up your insights and familiarity with what they're all about.

Apply. Keep asking yourself, *How does this truth affect my life?* (Pray for God's help as you examine yourself in light of that truth, and in light of His purpose for each passage.)

Try to consciously follow all three of these approaches as you shape your written answer to each question in the lesson.

The Extras

In addition to the regular numbered questions you see in this guide, each lesson also offers several optional questions or suggestions in the margins. All of these appear under one of three headings:

Optional Application. Try as many of these questions as you can without overcommitting yourself, considering them with prayerful sensitivity to the Lord's guidance.

For Thought and Discussion. Many of these questions address various ethical issues and other biblical principles that lead to a wide range of implications. They are well suited for group discussions.

For Further Study. These often include cross-references to other parts of the Bible that shed light on a topic in the lesson, plus questions that delve deeper into the passage.

(For additional help for more effective Bible study, refer to the "Study Aids" section beginning on page 151.)

Changing Your Life

Don't let your study become an exercise in knowledge alone. Treat the passage as God's Word, and stay in dialogue with Him as you study. Pray, "Lord, what do You want me to notice here?" "Father, why is this true?" "Lord, how does my life measure up to this?" Let biblical truth sink into your inner convictions so you'll increasingly be able to act on this truth as a natural way of living.

At times you may want to consider memorizing a certain verse or passage you come across in your study, one that particularly challenges or encourages you. To help with that, write down the words on a card to keep with you, and set aside a few minutes each day to think about the passage. Recite it to yourself repeatedly, always thinking about its meaning. Return to it as often as you can for a brief review. You'll soon find the words coming to mind spontaneously, and they'll begin to affect your motives and actions.

For Group Study

Exploring Scripture together in a group is especially valuable for the encouragement, support, and accountability it provides as you seek to apply God's Word to your life. Together you can listen for God's guidance, pray for each other, help one another resist temptation, and share the spiritual principles you're learning to put into practice. Together you affirm that growing in faith, hope, and love is important, and that *you need each other* in the process.

A group of four to ten people allows for the closest understanding of each other and the richest discussions in Bible study, but you can adapt this guide for other-sized groups. It will suit a wide range of group types, such as home Bible studies, growth groups, youth groups, and church classes. Both new and mature Christians will benefit from the guide, regardless of their previous experience in Bible study.

Aim for a positive atmosphere of acceptance, honesty, and openness. In your first meeting, explore candidly everyone's expectations and goals for your time together.

A typical schedule for group study is to take one lesson per week, but feel free to split lessons if you want to discuss them more thoroughly. Or omit some questions in a lesson if your preparation or discussion time is limited. (You can always return to this guide later for further study on your own.)

When you come together, you probably won't have time to discuss all the questions in the lesson, so it's helpful to choose ahead of time the ones you want to make sure and cover thoroughly. This is one of the main responsibilities that a group leader typically assumes.

Each lesson in this guide ends with a section called "For the Group." It gives advice for that particular lesson on how to focus the discussion, how to apply the lesson to daily life, and so on. Reading each lesson's "For the Group" section ahead of time can help the leader be more effective in guiding the group.

You'll get the greatest benefit from your time together if each group member prepares ahead of time by writing out his or her answers to each question in the lesson. The private reflection and prayer that this preparation can stimulate will be especially important in helping everyone discern how God wants you to apply each lesson to your daily lives.

There are many ways to structure the group meeting, and you may want to vary your routine occasionally to help keep things fresh.

Here are some elements you can consider including as you come together for each lesson:

Pray together. It's good to pause for prayer as you begin your time together. When you begin with prayer, it's worthwhile and honoring to God to ask especially for His Holy Spirit's guidance of your time together. If you write down each other's prayer requests, you are more likely to remember to pray for them during the week, ask about them at the next meeting, and notice answered prayers. You might want to get a notebook for prayer requests and discussion notes.

Worship. Some groups like to sing together and worship God with prayers of praise.

Review. You may want to take time to discuss what difference the previous week's lesson has made in your life, as well recall the major emphasis you discovered in the passage for that week.

Read the passage aloud. Once you're ready to focus attention together on the assigned Scripture passage in this week's lesson, read it aloud. (One person could this, or the reading could be shared.)

Open up for lingering questions. Allow time for the group members to mention anything in the passage that they may have particular questions about.

Summarize the passage. Have one or two persons summarize the passage.

Discuss. This will be the heart of your time together and will likely take the biggest portion of your time. Focus on the questions you see as the most important and most helpful. Allow and encourage everyone to be part of the discussion. You may want to take written notes as the discussion proceeds. Ask follow-up questions to sharpen your attention and to deepen your understanding of what you discuss. You may want to give special attention to the questions in the margin under the heading "For Thought and Discussion." Remember that sometimes these can be especially good for discussion, but be prepared for widely different answers and opinions. As you hear each other, keep in mind each other's various backgrounds, personalities, and ways of thinking. You can practice godly discernment without ungodly judgment in your discussion.

Encourage further personal study. You can find more opportunities for exploring this lesson's themes and issues under the marginal heading "For Further Study" throughout the lesson. You can also pursue some of these together, during your group time.

8

Focus on application. Look especially at the "Optional Application" items listed in the margins throughout the lesson. Keep encouraging one another in the continual work of adjusting our lives to the truths God gives us in Scripture.

Summarize your discoveries. You may want to read aloud through the passage one last time together, using this opportunity to solidify your understanding and appreciation of it and to clarify how the Lord is speaking to you through it.

Look ahead. Glance together at the headings and questions in the next lesson to see what's coming next.

Give thanks to God. It's good to end your time together by pausing to express gratitude to God for His Word and for the work of His Spirit in your minds and hearts.

Get to know each other better. In early sessions together, you may want to spend time establishing trust, common ground, a sense of each other's background, and what each person hopes to gain from the study. This may help you later with honest discussion on how the Bible applies to each of you. Understanding each other better will make it easier to share about personal applications.

Keep these worthy guidelines in mind throughout your time together:

Let us consider how we may spur one another on toward love and good deeds.

(HEBREWS 10:24)

Carry each other's burdens, and in this way you will fulfill the law of Christ.

(GALATIANS 6:2)

Accept one another, then, just as Christ accepted you, in order to bring praise to God.

(ROMANS 15:7)

9

THE BOOK OF JEREMIAH

Judgment and Hope

By worldly standards, the man Jeremiah "was a miserable failure. For forty years he served as God's spokesman to Judah; but when Jeremiah spoke, nobody listened. Consistently and passionately he urged them to act, but nobody moved. And he certainly did not attain material success. He was poor and underwent severe deprivation to deliver his prophecies. He was thrown into prison and into a well, and he was taken to Egypt against his will. He was rejected by his neighbors, his family, the false priests and prophets, friends, his audience, and the kings. Throughout his life, Jeremiah stood alone, declaring God's messages of doom, announcing the new covenant, and weeping over the fate of his beloved country. In the eyes of the world, Jeremiah was not a success.

"But in God's eyes, Jeremiah was one of the most successful people in all of history. Success, as measured by God, involves obedience and faithfulness. Regardless of opposition and personal cost, Jeremiah courageously and faithfully proclaimed the word of God. He was obedient to his calling."[1]

The Man Jeremiah

Jeremiah was a priest from the city of Anathoth (see Jeremiah 1:1; 11:21-23), in the land of the tribe of Benjamin. Anathoth was located about three miles northeast of Jerusalem, at the site of present-day Anata. Ancient Anathoth "was a walled town of some strength, seated on a broad ridge of hills and overlooking the valley of Jordan and the northern part of the Dead Sea."[2]

Jeremiah's ministry occurred about two centuries after that of Isaiah. He began his ministry in about the year 627 BC, and it continued for at least four decades.

"Jewish tradition says that the Jewish refugees stoned him to death in Egypt, because he criticized their life in exile."[3]

"He was the most autobiographical of all the prophets, and we know more about him than any other. . . . Jeremiah's life—private and public—is openly displayed in his book. His brave actions, his tenderheartedness toward

11

his coreligionists, his deep emotional and spiritual struggles before God—all these and more are clearly presented. His disappointments and sufferings were undeniably as poignant as those of any other Jewish prophet. . . . His life may be characterized as being one long martyrdom."[4]

Historical Background

In the history books of the Old Testament, the historical narrative of Jeremiah's time is given in 2 Kings 21–25 and 2 Chronicles 33–36. The prophets Zephaniah, Nahum, Habakkuk, and Ezekiel were also active around Jeremiah's time.

"The book of Jeremiah is so filled with historical, biographical, and auto-biographical material that his life can be synchronized with dates and known events to a degree unparalleled in the writings of other prophets."[5]

At the beginning of Jeremiah's ministry, the sudden decline of Assyrian power in the Middle East, along with the strong and reforming leadership of Judah's King Josiah, seemed to signal a positive future for God's people. "But the next generation was destined to experience the most catastrophic reversal of fortune in the nation's history, leading to ultimate destruction and captivity in 586 BC at the hands of the Neo-Babylonians, who by that time had emerged as the undisputed rulers of the ancient Near East. Into these turbulent and tragic times Jeremiah was called to be God's spokesman."[6]

Jeremiah's lifetime was "one of those tempestuous periods when the world at large goes into convulsion: in this case with Assyria's empire falling apart, and Egypt fighting in vain to keep Babylon from picking up the pieces—among which, ominously, was little Judah."[7]

"The book of Jeremiah is a tragedy. . . . It is about the unraveling of a nation. It is the sad story of the decline of God's people from faith to idolatry to exile."[8]

Jeremiah's Message

"Better than anyone else, Jeremiah reveals the spiritual fractures beneath the comfortable surface of daily life."[9]

"Jeremiah's message moved through phases that do not correspond exactly to the structure of the book:

"(a) He called Judah to repent and avoid judgment that would otherwise come.

"(b) He announced that the time for repentance was past, since judgment was now determined against the people. Judgment is the dominant note in the book, and is understood as the invocation of the final curse of the covenant, namely, loss of the Promised Land (Leviticus 26:31-33; Deuteronomy 28:49-68).

"(c) The Lord would save His people, or a remnant of them, through the exile. . . . This promise of eventual deliverance was Jeremiah's answer to the false prophets who had constantly challenged his message of judgment.

"Jeremiah also had a message of salvation, but only on the other side of judgment. That message is crystallized in the prophecy of the new covenant. The new covenant . . . speaks of the empowerment of God's people to obey Him. Although it is promised in national terms, it is something new, which the New Testament shows to be fulfilled in the greater 'Israel of God' (Galatians 6:16) through Christ."[10]

The Book's Style

Jeremiah's "discourses are like the frames of a moving picture; each presents the same characters but in slightly different positions. Indeed, the frames may be somewhat mixed up. Thus, the progression in the book is not straightforward and flowing. The transitions between the frames are abrupt and the repetitions frequent." Thus, Jeremiah "is sometimes charged with lack of originality, but this is a superficial judgment. The power of his imagination gives new depth and poignancy to the tradition out of which he speaks. His great poetical skill is seen especially in his vivid presentations of human loneliness and suffering. Jeremiah's poetry attains depths of pure emotion that reach every reader."[11]

"Jeremiah's poetry is lyrical; indeed, some would call him the greatest lyrical poet of all the prophets. His poetry consists of tender elegies, full of pathos. He has been termed 'the poet of the heart.' He uses imagery and figures with dramatic effect."[12]

"The leading characteristic of his style is a certain simplicity. His writing is direct, vivid, unornamented, incisive, and clear. Though not the lofty language of Isaiah, it has its own attractiveness. There is an unstudied truthfulness as the prophet's most intimate thoughts come pouring out of his anguished soul.

"Prominent in Jeremiah's style is the note of sorrow. With good reason he has been called the 'weeping prophet.' The plight of his people never left him, and he could not respond to it dispassionately. Among his writings are some of the most tender and sympathetic passages in the Bible. When he denounces, he does so with real anguish of soul. A vein of sorrow and sadness runs throughout the book. Touch the work where you will, and it will weep.

"Students of the prophecy observe Jeremiah's fondness for repetition. . . . This . . . is understandable in view of the sameness of the message God commanded him to preach. The people kept on in the same sins, and Jeremiah did not alter the penalty God required him to pronounce against them. If his style is occasionally monotonous, it is a style that reflects the tragic mood of his message. He leaves his readers with an inescapable impression of the monotony of sin and of its inevitable judgment."[13]

Jeremiah and Christ

"The life of no other prophet has so close an analogy to the earthly life of our Lord. Jeremiah has been rightly called the most Christlike of the prophets. Certain disciples saw in Jesus of Nazareth the prophet Jeremiah returned to life (Matthew 16:14). Here are some analogies between Jesus and Jeremiah:

"Their historical settings were similar. Jerusalem was about to fall; the temple was soon to be destroyed; religion was buried in formalism; there was need for emphasis on the spiritual life. . . .

"Both had a message for Israel and the world.

"Both were conscious of the world of nature about them and used many figures from it. . . .

"Both were conscious of their call from God.

"Both condemned the commercialism of temple worship and did so in a similar way (Jeremiah 7:11; Matthew 21:13).

"Both were accused of political treason.

"Both were tried, persecuted, and imprisoned.

"Both foretold the destruction of the temple (Jeremiah 7:14; Mark 13:2). . . .

"Both wept over Jerusalem (Jeremiah 9:1; Luke 19:41).

"Both forcefully condemned the priests of their day.

"Both were rejected by their kin (Jeremiah 12:6; John 1:11).

"Both were tenderhearted. . . .

"Both loved Israel deeply. . . .

"Both knew the meaning of loneliness (Jeremiah 15:10; Isaiah 53:3).

"Both enjoyed unusual fellowship with God. One of the unique features of Jeremiah's life was that he could be so free and honest in communion and conversation with God (Jeremiah 20:7; see John 11:41-42)."[14]

Structure of the Book

The book of Jeremiah contains more words than any other book in the Bible.

The arrangement of Jeremiah is thematic rather than strictly chronological. "Subject-matter counts for more than chronology in the arrangement of the book. . . . What he was given to say, rather than when it was said, must be our great concern."[15]

1. *Life Application Bible*, various editions (Wheaton, IL: Tyndale, 1988 and later), introduction to Jeremiah.
2. Merrill F. Unger, *New Unger's Bible Dictionary* (Chicago: Moody, 2006), s.v. "Anathoth."
3. J. I. Packer, Merrill C. Tenney, and William White Jr., eds., *Nelson's Illustrated Encyclopedia of Bible Facts* (Nashville: Thomas Nelson, 1995), 581.
4. Charles L. Feinberg, *Jeremiah*, The Expositor's Bible Commentary, vol. 6 (Grand Rapids, MI: Zondervan, 1986), 357–358.
5. Feinberg, 364.
6. Geoffrey W. Bromiley, ed., *International Standard Bible Encyclopedia*, vol. 2 (Grand Rapids, MI: Eerdmans, 1982), 985.

7. Derek Kidner, *The Message of Jeremiah*, The Bible Speaks Today (Downers Grove, IL: InterVarsity, 1987), 23.
8. Philip Graham Ryken, *Jeremiah and Lamentations: From Sorrow to Hope, Preaching the Word* (Wheaton, IL: Crossway, 2001), 26.
9. Ryken, 15.
10. *New Geneva Study Bible* (Nashville: Thomas Nelson, 1995), introduction to Jeremiah: "Characteristics and Themes."
11. Packer, Tenney, and White, 346.
12. Feinberg, 368.
13. Feinberg, 367–368.
14. Feinberg, 360–361.
15. Kidner, 29.

JEREMIAH 1–4

The Prophet's Calling and Message

1. For getting the most from Jeremiah, one of the best guidelines is found in 2 Timothy 3:16-17, words Paul wrote with the Old Testament first in view. He said that *all* Scripture is of great benefit to (a) teach us, (b) rebuke us, (c) correct us, and (d) train us in righteousness. Paul added that these Scriptures completely equip the person of God "for every good work." As you think seriously about those guidelines, in which of these areas do you especially want to experience the usefulness of Jeremiah? Express your desire in a written prayer to God.

_____

_____

_____

_____

2. Near the middle of this book of Jeremiah — in 23:29 — God says that His Word is like fire and like a hammer. He can use the Scriptures to burn away unclean thoughts and desires in our hearts. He can also use Scripture, with hammer-like hardness, to crush and crumble our spiritual hardness. From your study of Jeremiah, how do you most want to see the "fire-and-hammer" power of God's Word at work in your own life? Again, express this longing in a written prayer to God.

Optional Application: After His resurrection, when Jesus was explaining Old Testament passages to His disciples, He "opened their minds so they could understand the Scriptures" (Luke 24:45). Ask God to do that kind of work in *your* mind as you study Jeremiah, so you're released and free to learn everything here He wants you to learn — and so you can become as bold and worshipful and faithful as those early disciples of Jesus were. Express this desire to Him in prayer.

_____

_____

_____

3. Think about these words of Paul to his younger
   helper Timothy: "Do your best to present yourself to God as one approved, a worker who does
   not need to be ashamed and who correctly han-
   dles the word of truth" (2 Timothy 2:15). As you
   study God's word of truth in Jeremiah, he calls
   you to be a "worker." It takes _work_—concentra-
   tion and perseverance—to fully appropriate
   God's blessings for us in this book. Express here
   your commitment before God to work diligently
   in this study of Jeremiah.

_____

_____

_____

4. Glance ahead throughout the pages of
   Jeremiah. If your Bible includes topic headings,
   note all of these. Allow your eyes also to take in
   any particular phrases or sentences in the text
   that catch your attention. What are your overall
   impressions of this book?

_____

_____

_____

A Moving and Powerful Message
In the first half of this book, Jeremiah "labors to
develop the theme of national sinfulness from
the statement of the prophet's credentials to
the final judgment. As a unit it forms a somewhat disjointed whole with varying kinds of
literary forms interwoven: oracles of hope and
doom and autobiographical, biographical, and
conversational (dialogue) narrative.... Thus he

interweaves and repeats the theme of national
sinfulness and coming judgment, often going
back over material already presented, as a
fugue does in music. The effect is powerful and
moving."[1]

5. In one sitting if possible, read attentively
   through all of Jeremiah 1–4, taking notes and
   underlining or highlighting as you go. What
   impresses you overall as the key features and
   themes of this part of the book?

   _____

   _____

   _____

The word of the Lord came to me, saying . . .
     (1:4). "This verse is the heart of the prophetic
     experience."[2]

6. What do chapters 1–4 reveal most about God's
   heart for His people and His relationship with
   His people?

   _____

   _____

   _____

7. What do these chapters identify most clearly
   and specifically as Israel's wrongdoing? What
   exactly were God's people most guilty of, and
   most in need of repentance for?

   _____

   _____

   _____

   _____

8. In particular, how would you summarize what these chapters teach us about the sin of idolatry?

_____

_____

_____

9. What do these opening chapters of Jeremiah teach us most about repentance, from God's perspective?

_____

_____

_____

10. Verses 2 and 3 of Jeremiah 1 mention the kings under whose reigns Jeremiah lived and ministered. What are the most important things you already know about these kings and their reigns?

_____

_____

_____

"The three kings named here [in 1:2-3], Josiah the reformer, Jehoiakim the tyrant, and Zedekiah the weathercock, touched three extremes of royal character that created changes in the spiritual climate which were fully as violent as those of the political scene."[3]

In the thirteenth year of the reign of Josiah (1:2). This "was one year after the beginning of that king's reformation movement (2 Chronicles 34:3)."[4] This time of Jeremiah's call also "coincided approximately with the death of the last great Assyrian ruler, Ashurbanipal, an event

20

which signaled the disintegration of the Assyrian empire under whose yoke Judah had served for nearly a century. Against the waning power and influence of the Assyrians, Judah asserted its independence under Josiah, and for a time the prospects for a secure national future appeared promising."[5]

11. As the Lord calls Jeremiah to ministry in 1:4-19, what do you see as the most important things the Lord communicates to Jeremiah — and the things that will be most valuable for him to remember throughout his ministry?

_____

_____

_____

I appoint you . . . to uproot and tear down, to destroy and overthrow, to build and to plant (1:10). "The prophet's job description includes six tasks, and four of them are negative. Two to one, his words to the nations will be words of judgment. . . . This verse is not only Jeremiah's job description, it is also a helpful plot-summary of his book. He lives in such evil days that judgment will outnumber grace two to one."[7]

A pot that is boiling . . . tilting toward us from the north (1:13). This "seething cauldron, tilting dangerously as the fire settled, made a terribly appropriate picture of the menace from the north (the old invasion route of Assyria, soon to be that of Babylon); and it remains as apt as ever to the human scene where, from one quarter after another, human aggressiveness lets loose a scalding stream of havoc."[8]

Get yourself ready! . . . I have made you a fortified city. . . . I am with you and will rescue you (1:17-19). "Jeremiah is given strong encouragement for his hard task, because his message would be neither welcome nor popular with his people. To fulfill his duties, nothing less than utter commitment to God and to his

For Further Study:
What do you see as the highlights of the reign of King Josiah (who's mentioned in Jeremiah 1:2), as you find his reign narrated in 2 Kings 22–23 and 2 Chronicles 34–35? Note especially the reforms Josiah fostered. "There can be little doubt that this national repentance warmed the heart of the young prophet [Jeremiah], and for a time at least he may have actively supported the reformation by speaking on behalf of its ideals (see Jeremiah 11:1-8, which may be derived from this period). . . . The condition of Jeremiah under Josiah was probably the happiest of his career."[6]

21

For Thought and Discussion: What truths and principles from Jeremiah's calling (in chapter 1) do you see as especially applicable to Christian preachers and teachers today?

Optional Application: How does Jeremiah's calling relate to your own calling in life — to what God has called you to do? What are the similarities? What are the differences?

strength would suffice. With God, Jeremiah would be invincible. In his darkest hours these words sustained him mentally, emotionally, and spiritually."[9]

12. How do you especially see God's grace, protection, and provision for Jeremiah coming through in chapter 1?

_____

_____

_____

_____

_____

Worthless (2:5). Their worthlessness involved "exchanging the real for the unreal, the eternal for the ephemeral. 'Worthlessness' here is hebel, the 'vanity' of Ecclesiastes 1:2, etc."[10]

In 2:1-3, "there is the freshness of spring in the Lord's first words to Israel, recapturing the ardor of young love — that readiness of the beloved to go anywhere, put up with anything, so long as it could be shared with her partners. . . . To begin on such a note was the way to awaken any spark of longing or compunction that might still lie dormant in the hearers (for affection can disarm us where a scolding only rankles). . . . Whatever else was wrong with Israel — and there was no lack of it — the violated marriage was fundamental."[11]

Those who deal with the law did not know me; the leaders rebelled against me (2:8). "A holy calling does not make a holy man. The priests of Jeremiah's day were handling the Scriptures, studying the Bible, and teaching God's Word, but they did not know God himself (see John 5:39-40). Their ministry was a dead ritual rather than a living relationship."[12]

22

Broken cisterns that cannot hold water (2:13).
"The best cisterns, even those in solid rock, are
strangely liable to crack . . ., and if by constant
care they are made to hold, yet the water collected from clay roofs or from marly soil has
the color of weak soapsuds, the taste of the
earth or the stable, is full of worms, and in the
hour of greatest need it utterly fails."[13]

***On your clothes is found the lifeblood of the
innocent poor*** (2:34). "With God dethroned,
nothing is unthinkable: not even murder —
here quite literally, since the regime of King
Manasseh (in whose reign Jeremiah was born)
had 'filled Jerusalem from one end to another
with innocent blood' (2 Kings 21:16; to which
we may add the question, What of our own
society's murders of convenience? What is
more innocent than an embryo?)"[14]

13. What do you see as the particular messianic
significance of the promises in Jeremiah 3:14-
17?

_____

_____

_____

_____

_____

***Return, faithless people . . . for I am your hus-
band*** (3:14). "That is the divine call, the free
invitation of God to come to him for salvation.
It is the free offer of the gospel that is offered to
all men, women, and children in Jesus Christ.
But notice what the Lord goes on to say." I will
choose you — one from a town and two from
a clan — and bring you to Zion (3:14). "That is
divine election, God's choice. God's choosing
stands behind God's calling."[16]

For Further Study:
In Jeremiah 2:21, God
speaks of His people
as "a choice vine" that
He has planted. How
is this image of God's
people further devel-
oped in the following
passages? Psalm 80:8-
15; Isaiah 5:1-7; Ezekiel
15:1-8; John 15:1-11.

For Further Study:
As further back-
ground on God's
question about
divorce in Jeremiah
3:1, what do you
learn from the
regulations given in
Deuteronomy 24:1-
4? "This law, which
forbade a divorced
couple to reunite,
was aimed against
what would amount
to virtually lend-
ing one's partner to
another — for if an
authoritarian hus-
band could dismiss
his wife and have her
back when the next
man had finished
with her, it would
degrade not only
her but marriage
itself and the society
that accepted such a
practice."[15]

"Now, surprisingly, God presses home the point by a change of tone from judgment to grace.... Notice the great vista opened up in verses 15-18. Characteristically, God is not content with short-term answers to a crisis, but looks on to perfection.... What is said here of the shepherds (i.e., rulers) and of the ark and the nations reveals the scale of this transformation, with God's people ideally governed (3:15), his earthly throne no longer a mere ark but his entire city (note the astonishing boldness of verse 16); his Jerusalem the rallying point of all nations, now converted; and his divided Israel home and reunited. It brings us right into the era of the new covenant, and indeed to the new heavens and earth and the 'New Jerusalem' of Revelation 21–22, whose 'temple is the Lord God' (Revelation 21:22), and whose open gates admit 'the glory and honor of the nations' (Revelation 21:26).

"If so distant a prospect was worth unveiling to the old Israel, six centuries before Christ, it must be doubly relevant to us who have reached its foothills."[17]

14. From chapter 4 of Jeremiah, how would you summarize the warnings given by the Lord to His people?

_____

_____

_____

"The visions come thick and fast in chapter 4, bombarding us with the terrors of invasion."[18]

"Jeremiah 4 is a living nightmare of divine judgment. The terrible things that befall Judah for refusing to turn back to God are jumbled all together."[19]

Break up your unplowed ground and do not sow among thorns (4:3). "He exhorts the people of Judah to break up their neglected and untilled hearts, which had become as hard as an uncultivated field. . . . The plow of repentance and obedience was needed to remove the outer layer of weeds and thorns that had resulted from idolatry."[20]

Circumcise your hearts (4:4). "The hard encrustation on their hearts must be cut away. Nothing less than removal of all natural obstacles to the will of God would suffice. Outward ritual must be replaced by inward reality (see Deuteronomy 10:16; Romans 2:28-29)."[21]

I said, "Alas, Sovereign LORD! How completely you have deceived this people . . ." (4:10). "It is the first of many glimpses into his troubled mind; and his surprise at his own vision of verses 5-9 chimes in with the New Testament's dictum that such prophecies came not by the impulse of man but from God (2 Peter 1:20-21)."[22]

They know not how to do good (4:22). "Good, in Scripture, is not only plain and simple ('very near,' Deuteronomy 30:14); it has heights and depths which we must be taught even to see (as in, for example, the Sermon on the Mount) and inspired to love and do."[23]

"Jeremiah's psalm style is especially evident in his second psalm of lamentation (Jeremiah 4:19-31)."[24]

25

For Thought and Discussion: What are your impressions so far of the man Jeremiah? How would you describe his personality and character?

I looked at the earth, and it was formless and empty; and at the heavens, and their light was gone (4:23). "While the Genesis story was all expectancy, this is the opposite: an abandonment, a reversion, and a divine unmaking . . . (4:25-26)."[25] In 4:23-26, "the striking repetition of 'I looked' . . . ties this poem together and underscores its visionary character, as the prophet sees his beloved land in ruins after the Babylonian onslaught. Creation, as it were, has been reversed."[26]

I will not destroy it completely. (4:27). Notice how this promise is repeated at 5:10,18 and with particular emphasis at 30:11. This statement "shines very brightly. It is a constant theme, not only here but throughout the prophets. Without it the Old Testament would not have been worth writing, and the New Testament would never have materialized. Its context here [in 4:23-27] of a silent, devastated world makes the point that only God's 'Yet . . .' has rescued or will rescue anything at all from the battlefield that we have made of his creation."[27] Here we see both God's wrath as well as His mercy—and "both of these . . . reflect his intense commitment to us—both the seriousness with which he takes us and the determination to complete the work of grace that he has begun."[28]

15. What would you select as the key verse or passage in Jeremiah 1–4—one that best captures or reflects the dynamics of what these chapters are all about?

_____

_____

_____

_____

16. List any lingering questions you have about Jeremiah 1–4.

26

_____

_____

_____

_____

Optional Application: On the basis of God's truth revealed in Jeremiah 1–4, perhaps the Holy Spirit has helped you sense a new and higher reality in your life that God is inviting you to. If this is true for you, express in your own words the reality that you long for, and use it as a springboard for prayer.

For the Group

In your first meeting, it may be helpful to turn to the front of this book and review together the "How to Use This Study" section.

You may want to focus your discussion for lesson 1 especially on the following core biblical concepts, all of which are dealt with extensively in Jeremiah. (These themes will likely reflect what group members have learned in their individual study of this week's passage—though they'll also have made discoveries in other areas as well.)

- sin
- judgment
- repentance
- grace
- salvation

The following numbered questions in lesson 1 may stimulate your best and most helpful discussion: 4, 5, 6, 9, 12, 13, 15, and 16.

Look also at the questions in the margins under the heading "For Thought and Discussion."

1. J. I. Packer, Merrill C. Tenney, and William White Jr., eds., *Nelson's Illustrated Encyclopedia of Bible Facts* (Nashville: Thomas Nelson, 1995), 346.
2. Charles L. Feinberg, *Jeremiah*, The Expositor's Bible Commentary, vol. 6 (Grand Rapids, MI: Zondervan, 1986), 383.
3. Derek Kidner, *The Message of Jeremiah*, The Bible Speaks Today (Downers Grove, IL: InterVarsity, 1987), 23–24.
4. Kidner, 29.
5. Geoffrey W. Bromiley, ed., *International Standard Bible Encyclopedia*, vol. 2 (Grand Rapids, MI: Eerdmans, 1982), 985.
6. Bromiley, 985.
7. Philip Graham Ryken, *Jeremiah and Lamentations: From Sorrow to Hope,* Preaching the Word (Wheaton, IL: Crossway, 2001), 26.

8. Kidner, 27.
9. Feinberg, 386.
10. Kidner, 31.
11. Kidner, 30.
12. Ryken, 40.
13. W. M. Thomson, *The Land and the Book* (New York: Harper, 1886), 287; in Kidner, 32.
14. Kidner, 34.
15. Kidner, 35.
16. Ryken, 55.
17. Kidner, 36–37.
18. Kidner, 39.
19. Ryken, 73.
20. Feinberg, 405.
21. Feinberg, 405.
22. Kidner, 42.
23. Kidner, 42.
24. Packer, Tenney, and White, 346.
25. Kidner, 40.
26. *NIV Study Bible* (Grand Rapids, MI: Zondervan, 1985), on Jeremiah 4:23-26.
27. Kidner, 43.
28. Kidner, 40–41.

JEREMIAH 5–10

The Message of Judgment Intensified

1. In one sitting if possible, read attentively through all of Jeremiah 5–10, taking notes and underlining or highlighting as you go. What impresses you overall as the key features and themes of this part of the book?

   _____

   _____

   _____

2. From what you see here (as well as in the earlier chapters of Jeremiah), how would you describe the nature and personality of God's people? From God's perspective, what characteristics of His people are most significant?

   _____

   _____

   _____

   _____

3. From what you see in these chapters, what are the most significant consequences for Israel's sins?

   _____

   _____

4. Especially from chapter 5, what would you say are the big reasons for Israel's refusal to repent?

_____

_____

_____

Chapter 5 "reveals Jerusalem under moral investigation. . . . The nation must come to a much fuller realization of her ingrained sin. The desperately low spiritual state of the nation must be brought under the searchlight of God's scrutiny. Moreover, her sin must be judged in view of her continued refusal to heed the Lord's gracious calls to repent and to avert disaster. What a telling portrayal of unrelieved apostasy the chapter gives us!"[1]

5. God asks His people (in 5:7), "Why should I forgive you?" Express in your own words what you see as the essential theological answer to that question, both in regard to God's people in Jeremiah's day, and in regard to us today.

_____

_____

_____

As you have forsaken me and served foreign gods in your own land, so now you will serve foreigners in a land not your own (5:19). "God could hardly be any more fair! The people of Jerusalem had worshiped foreign gods all along. What could be more appropriate than sending them to a place where they could serve those gods to their hearts' content? Be careful what you desire: God might grant it!"[2]

"In chapters 5 and 6 … God builds up the case against his people."[3]

6. Chapter 6 of Jeremiah intensifies the picture of God's rejection of His people. What are the most important truths they needed to understand about this rejection?

_____

_____

_____

> In chapter 6, "the striking feature … is its rapidity of movement leading to the gathering storm of invasion soon to engulf the capital and the land. It has been called a chapter of alarms; it begins on a note of impending doom and concludes with the utter rejection of the people."[4]

Their ears are closed so they cannot hear (6:10). "Jerusalem's wickedness is the sin of a closed mind."[5]

They have no shame at all (6:15). "The closed mind produces a calloused conscience."[6]

7. What particular significance do you see in the Lord's instruction in 6:16?

_____

_____

_____

Stand at the crossroads and look (6:16). "People had lost all sense of direction. They were disoriented. They groped in bewilderment and wandered in the dark. They needed a landmark. So Jeremiah gave them one. This is a verse for

For Further Study: Compare the rebelliousness of God's people that you read about in Jeremiah 5:21-23 with what you see in these passages: Deuteronomy 9:7,24; 31:27; Psalm 78:40; Isaiah 6:9-10; 30:1,9; 65:2; Ezekiel 12:2; Daniel 9:5-9; Acts 7:51-52.

For Further Study: The Lord tells His people in 6:16 how to "find rest for your souls." Explore this phrase as Jesus used it in Matthew 11:25-30. How does this New Testament context expand the full biblical meaning of this phrase?

For Further Study:
Compare the biblical concept of prophetic "watchmen" (Jeremiah 6:17; see also 31:5-6) with what you observe in these passages: Isaiah 21:6-12; 62:6-7; Ezekiel 3:16-21. Also, in the New Testament, how is this function served by church leaders, according to the instruction in Acts 20:28-31 and Hebrews 13:17?

Optional Application: Look again at the Lord's directive to His people in Jeremiah 6:16. How do you see this applying to believers today? How does it apply to you?

For Further Study:
With Jeremiah 6:27-30 in mind, explore the image of the fire of refinement and the fire of judgment in the following passages, and describe what you learn: Isaiah 1:21-31; 48:10; Ezekiel 22:17-22; Malachi 3:2-3.

people who have come to the crossroads and do not know which way to turn."[7]

You said, 'We will not walk in it.' . . . 'We will not listen' (6:16-17). "It is a shock to find that these are studiously religious people, sparing no expense to offer God the best of everything ["incense from Sheba . . . sweet calamus from a distant land," 6:20] — everything, that is, but love. . . . We may wonder whether it has any modern counterpart—whether, for example, our own religiousness is conceivably as cold as Judah's, to provoke again God's penetrating question of verse 20 (NEB): 'What good is it to me . . . ?'"[8]

Look, an army is coming from the land of the north. . . . They are cruel and show no mercy. . . . Anguish has gripped us (6:22-24). Almost the exact wording of these three verses "will meet us again at the end of the book, spoken no longer against Judah but against Babylon itself! — for God is no respecter of persons or powers. See 50:41-43."[9]

Is terror on every side (6:25). "A phrase that will reverberate through the book and on into Lamentations."[10] See 20:3-4,10; 46:5; 49:29; Lamentations 2:22.

As Jeremiah 7 opens, we see the start of what is called Jeremiah's great temple sermon, as God tells him, "Stand at the gate of the LORD's house and there proclaim this message" (7:2). The sermon appears to extend through 8:3 and possibly through all of chapters 7–10. This proclamation "has been called one of the majestic scenes of history. One of the crucial events in his ministry, it undoubtedly initiated the unrelenting opposition he experienced during the remainder of his life."[11]

Later, Jeremiah 26 "records the consequences of the address. The time was not long after the death of Josiah. The entire discourse seemed to run counter to Josiah's attempt to centralize worship at the temple in Jerusalem and appeared to blast hopes inculcated by the earlier prophets, Isaiah among them. Josiah's reform promised a restoration of God's blessing and not the calamity of the temple and the dissolution of the commonwealth. In Isaiah's day the repentance of godly Hezekiah and the people issued in God's removal of the Assyrian threat in one night (Isaiah 37:36). But the spiritual decline of the nation proved irreversible in Jeremiah's time."[12]

"While chapter 26 concentrates on the effect of the sermon on the hearers, chapter 7 is concerned with its contents in full, which clinch the predictions and reproaches of the previous chapters. The two sermons, or the two accounts of one sermon, complement and reinforce one another, pointing on to the blow which fell surely enough in 587 B.C."[13]

8. Chapters 7–10 of Jeremiah "give evidence of the truth of God's accusations in chapters 2–6."[14] What is that evidence, as you see it in these chapters? (Summarize this in your own words.)

_____

_____

_____

9. God says to His people (in 7:3), "Reform your ways and your actions." From what you observe in these chapters, what did this reforming need to involve?

_____

_____

_____

The place in Shiloh where I first made a dwelling for my Name (7:12). See Psalm 78:60. Shiloh "was the central sanctuary (about 19 miles north of Jerusalem) prior to the monarch (Judges 21:19; 1 Samuel 1:3)."[15] "If God's people went to Shiloh in Jeremiah's day, they

For Further Study:
As you reflect on what God says about burnt offerings and sacrifices in Jeremiah 7:22-23, what comparison and connection do you notice with the following passages: Psalm 40:6-8; Isaiah 1:11-17; Hosea 6:6; Amos 5:21-24; Micah 6:6-8?

For Further Study:
Jeremiah 7:31 refers to Israel's despicable practice of child-sacrifice. What do you learn about this abomination in these passages: 2 Kings 16:3; 21:6; Jeremiah 19:5; 32:35; Ezekiel 16:20-21.

would not find God or God's living presence, but only a pile of rubble. The archaeological evidence shows that Shiloh was destroyed twice over—once by the Philistines and once when the Assyrians carried the northern tribes into captivity. When Jeremiah told the people to go to Shiloh, he was telling them to go to the place where God is not. Shiloh is the place where God once was and is no longer. . . . Shiloh thus represents the absence and abandonment of God along with the end of his worship."[16]

Do not pray for this people (7:16). See the similar instruction in 11:14 and 14:11.

Children . . . fathers . . . women (7:18). "The glimpse in verse 18 of whole families assiduously worshiping the queen of heaven shows how deeply pagan was the folk-religion of the time. No minor surgery would touch it."[17]

I did not just give them commands about burnt offerings and sacrifices (7:22). "At first sight God seems to be disowning the whole idea of sacrifice. . . . But in fact this way of speaking is the Bible's strongest way of comparing one thing with another—here, the moral with the formal—putting it not in the mild form of 'This is better than that,' but with the starkness of 'Not that, but this!'"[18]

To burn their sons and daughters in the fire (7:31). "The indictment reaches a new intensity—which is saying something, after the catalogue of broken commandments in verse 9!—with the crowning horror of child-sacrifice. What is most revealing, however, about the pagan outlook is the fact that this was thought to be a crowning piety. The very carefulness of God's repudiation of it—which I did not command, nor did it come into my mind (verse 31)—tells its own tale of his people's darkened outlook."[19]

Valley of Ben Hinnom (7:32). In Hebrew, *gê' ben-hinnom*—"whose shortened name *gehenna* meets us as the New Testament's word for hell."[20]

10. How does 8:4-17 reveal the intensity of the people's sin?

_____

_____

_____

"If all this (in 8:4-17) emphasized the iron necessity of judgment, the ensuing stanzas (8:18–9:3) bring out the pathos of it, in a mingling of cries from the prophet, the people, and the Lord."[21]

The harvest is past, the summer has ended, and we are not saved (8:20). "The futility of their situation is summarized in one of the saddest verses in the Old Testament."[22]

Is there no balm in Gilead? Is there no physician there? Why then is there no healing for the wound of my people? (8:22). "The answer to these questions is that as long as God's people are dead in their trespasses and sins, there is no health in them. But once their sin is cleansed and their sins are forgiven, then all of God's promises will come true."[23]

---

11. What verses in chapter 9 convey most to you the grief felt by Jeremiah and by the Lord, and the reasons for it?

_____

_____

_____

Death has climbed in through our windows (9:21). "These paragraphs [in 9:7-22] spare us nothing of the desolation, the scattering, the weeping, and the horror of a massacre, where,

For Further Study:
How is God's intention and attitude in Jeremiah 8:1-3 reflected also in Leviticus 26:30 and Ezekiel 6:3-5?

For Further Study:
How would you compare Jeremiah's emotions in Jeremiah 9:1 with Paul's in Romans 9:1-5 and 10:1? With David's in 2 Samuel 18:33? With those of Jesus in Matthew 23:37?

For Thought and Discussion: How do our most common idols today compare with those of Jeremiah's day, as spoken against in these chapters of Jeremiah?

For Further Study: Jeremiah 9:25-26 speaks of those who are "who are circumcised only in the flesh" and "uncircumcised in heart." How do you see this theme further developed in the following passages? Leviticus 26:40-42; Deuteronomy 10:16; 30:6; Jeremiah 4:4; Romans 2:28-29; Galatians 6:12-15; Philippians 3:3; Colossians 2:11-15.

in a macabre metaphor, death not only prowls the streets but climbs the very windows; and where the fields too are strewn with his unnatural harvest."[24]

12. What do you see as the particular significance of 9:23-24, both for God's people in Jeremiah's day, and for believers today?

_____

_____

_____

Let the one who boasts boast about this: that they have the understanding to know me (9:24). "If you must boast—as all human beings must, because we were made to boast—then boast about the understanding and knowledge of God. Your boast is not that you understand and know God. The only reason you know God is because he has revealed himself through his Word and his world. But you may boast about God himself. The Christian's proper boast is in a Godward direction."[25]

13. Summarize how chapter 10 deepens our understanding of the Lord's perspective on idolatry.

_____

_____

_____

In chapter 10, "Jeremiah shows his firsthand knowledge of idol worship, both Canaanite and Babylonian. . . . Once men lose their awareness of God, they do not thereby lose their need of God. So they substitute the false worship for the true. Idolatry is the result."[26]

*Like a scarecrow in a cucumber field, their idols
cannot speak. . . . No one is like you, LORD;
you are great, and your name is mighty in
power* (10:5-6). "God is one-of-a-kind, incomparable. . . . Idols are a dime a dozen. There are as many idols as there are scarecrows in all the cucumber patches in the world. But there is only one God, whom Jeremiah presented as the One and Only. Idols are worthless, vain, empty. They cannot even stand on their own two feet without wobbling. But God is great. Even his name is mighty in power."[27]

14. What truths about God are emphasized in 10:6-10, and what is their significance for God's people in all ages?

_____

_____

_____

_____

_____

15. What particular insight into Jeremiah's heart and mind do you see in 10:23-24?

_____

_____

_____

_____

16. What would you select as the key verse or passage in Jeremiah 5–10 — one that best captures or reflects the dynamics of what these chapters are all about?

_____

_____

_____

_____

Optional Application: In Jeremiah's words in 10:23-24, what example do you see for the way you understand and value the correction and discipline you receive from the Lord? Express this in your own words, preferably as a prayer to the Lord.

For Thought and Discussion: What further impressions do you have of the man Jeremiah, of his personality and character?

Optional Application: On the basis of God's truth revealed in Jeremiah 5–10, perhaps the Holy Spirit has helped you sense a new and higher reality in your life that God is inviting you to. If this is true for you, express in your own words the reality that you long for, and use it as a springboard for prayer.

17. List any lingering questions you have about Jeremiah 5–10.

_____

_____

_____

For the Group

You may want to focus your discussion for lesson 2 especially on the following core biblical concepts, all of which are dealt with extensively in Jeremiah. (These themes will likely reflect what group members have learned in their individual study of this week's passage — though they'll also have made discoveries in other areas as well.)

- sin
- judgment
- repentance
- grace
- salvation

The following numbered questions in lesson 2 may stimulate your best and most helpful discussion: 1, 2, 6, 9, 12, 13, 14, 16, and 17.

Look also at the questions in the margins under the heading "For Thought and Discussion."

1. Charles L. Feinberg, *Jeremiah*, The Expositor's Bible Commentary, vol. 6 (Grand Rapids, MI: Zondervan, 1986), 411.
2. Philip Graham Ryken, *Jeremiah and Lamentations: From Sorrow to Hope,* Preaching the Word (Wheaton, IL: Crossway, 2001), 92.
3. Derek Kidner, *The Message of Jeremiah*, The Bible Speaks Today (Downers Grove, IL: InterVarsity, 1987), 39.
4. Feinberg, 419.
5. Kidner, 45.
6. Kidner, 46.
7. Ryken, 107.
8. Kidner, 46–47.
9. Kidner, 47.
10. Kidner, 47.
11. Feinberg, 426.
12. Feinberg, 426.

13. Kidner, 48.
14. *ESV Study Bible* (Wheaton, IL: Crossway, 2008), on Jeremiah 7–10.
15. *ESV Study Bible*, on Jeremiah 7:12-14.
16. Ryken, 125–126.
17. Kidner, 50.
18. Kidner, 50.
19. Kidner, 51.
20. Kidner, 51.
21. Kidner, 53.
22. Ryken, 165.
23. Ryken, 503.
24. Kidner, 55.
25. Ryken, 178.
26. Feinberg, 446.
27. Ryken, 189.

LESSON THREE

JEREMIAH 11–14
Dialogues with God

1. In one sitting if possible, read attentively through all of Jeremiah 11–14, taking notes and underlining or highlighting as you go. What impresses you overall as the key features and themes of this part of the book?

_____

_____

_____

For Thought and Discussion: What comes to mind when you think of God's "covenant" with His people? What should we understand most about this?

2. Chapter 11 begins with a look at the way the people of Israel broke their covenant with God. How did they fall short in their understanding and their application of that covenant?

_____

_____

_____

3. What reaction to Jeremiah and his message from the people in his hometown (Anathoth) is indicated in 11:18-23, and what reactions and responses do you see from Jeremiah and from the Lord?

_____

_____

_____

41

For Further Study:
In Jeremiah 11, God speaks of the "curses of the covenant" (11:8), and He says, "Cursed is the one who does not obey the terms of this covenant" (11:3). What should we understand about this biblical concept of "curse"? Let the following passages help you understand it: Genesis 3:14,17; Leviticus 26:14-43; Deuteronomy 11:26-28; 27:26; 28:15-68; 29:18-21; Joshua 23:13-15; Psalm 37:22; Proverbs 3:33; Isaiah 24:4-6; Jeremiah 23:10; Malachi 2:1-3; 3:6-12; Matthew 25:41-46; Galatians 3:10,13.

For Further Study:
Jeremiah speaks in 11:19 of being "like a gentle lamb led to the slaughter." Compare and contrast this with what you see of Christ in Isaiah 53:7; Acts 8:30-35; and 1 Peter 2:21-24.

For Thought and Discussion: In Jeremiah 12:1, the prophet asks God, "Why does the way of the wicked prosper? Why do all the faithless live at ease?" If you were asked those questions, how would you answer?

Let me see your vengeance upon them (11:20). Jeremiah's "fierce reaction to the plot will shock us; but God upheld it, for it asked no more than justice."[1] "Jeremiah's calls for revenge on his enemies . . . are explicable on the same basis as those in the Psalms, and should be understood as involving no feeling of personal vindictiveness. Jeremiah knew he was God's messenger; therefore, those who attacked him were arraying themselves against God. Jeremiah's intense fidelity to his God and his longing for the triumph of divine righteousness show that his curses were not so much personal as uttered for the vindication of the glory of the Lord."[2]

4. Summarize what is communicated in the interchange between Jeremiah and the Lord in Jeremiah 12, and what it reveals about each of them.

_____

_____

_____

_____

Why does the way of the wicked prosper? (12:1). "This is one of many cries of 'Why?' and 'How long?' in the Old Testament — to which God's answer is never philosophical, as though he owed us explanations, but always pastoral, to rebuke us, reorientate us, or reassure us. Here [in Jeremiah 12], when we include the long view of the closing verses (14-17), there will be something of all three."[3] "Jeremiah deals with the question of the prosperity of the wicked, which has been called the great problem of the Old Testament. Jeremiah's perplexity, and that of others like him, is understandable because the Old Testament does not offer full information on life after death. Only through the New Testament revelation, especially that of the resurrection of Christ (1 Peter 1:3-5), can the problem be placed in true perspective."[4]

How can you compete . . . ? How will you man-age . . . ? (12:5). "God does not always answer our questions. Usually he doesn't. In fact, in Jeremiah's case he came back with a few questions of his own."[5] "The sensitive Jeremiah rose to the challenge, not without loud cries of protest in the course of the next eight or nine chapters (sometimes called his 'Confessions,' sometimes his 'Gethsemane'). The result of this hard training can be seen in his fortitude, right through to the end of his comfortless career."[6]

5. Think about the gravity of the news the Lord tells Jeremiah in 12:6, and how it would impact him. If you were in Jeremiah's place, what do you think the impact would be? How would you describe it?

_____

_____

_____

Wicked neighbors (12:14). The nations around Judah.

6. How would you summarize the Lord's promise given in 12:14-17 to the nations nearby Judah?

_____

_____

_____

If they learn well . . . then they will be estab-lished among my people. But if any nation does not listen, I will completely uproot and destroy it (12:16-17). "The unexpected promise of Jeremiah 12:14-17 is the promise of paradise regained. . . . But universal salvation was already ruled out in the Old Testament. Even in Jeremiah 12, a prophecy about the

For Further Study: In Jeremiah 12, Jeremiah begins his prayer of complaint by acknowledging the Lord's righteous-ness. What should believers understand about the Lord's righ-teousness? Use these passages to help you form an answer in full: Deuteronomy 32:4; Ezra 9:15; Psalms 51:4; 119:137; 145:17; Lamentations 1:18; Daniel 9:7; Zephaniah 3:5.

For Thought and Discussion: When is it right and accept-able to complain to God? Or is it ever?

Optional Application: If God now asked you the questions He asked His prophet in Jeremiah 12:5, how would you answer? Think about the essence of what the Lord wants Jeremiah to understand here — what signifi-cance might it have for you in your own calling from God?

43

salvation of all nations, salvation was not for everyone. God's mercy is given freely but not universally. His salvation is wide, but it is not boundless. Can unbelievers be saved? Yes, but only if they become believers! The condition for entering into blessing with the people of God is swearing by God's name. The grace of God is available to all the nations of the world. Yet it is only given to those who come to the one true God and confess his name. What will happen if the nations do not swear by the name of God? Quite simply, they will not be saved."[7]

7. What themes and warnings do you see communicated in the various sections of chapter 13, and how do these tie together as a picture of Judah's future?

_____

_____

_____

_____

The various warnings in chapter 13 "reiterate the subjects on which Jeremiah has been preaching: sin and punishment."[8]

Go now to Perath (13:4). Or, "go to the Euphrates" (ESV). "In other contexts the Hebrew for Perath refers to the river Euphrates."[9] "Whether this was a literal journey, twice over, to the distant river Euphrates, or a journey of the mind (like some of Ezekiel's experiences), its point was very clear."[10]

For as a belt is bound around the waist, so I bound all the people of Israel and the people of Judah to me (13:11). "God used the linen belt to make the spiritual point that the best had become the worst. . . . The linen belt was meant to be a beautiful picture of God's relationship with his people. God wants us to be

44

bright and clean. He wants to wrap us around his waist like an embrace."[11]

I will weep in secret because of your pride; my eyes will weep bitterly (13:17). "There is all the difference between this attitude and that of the merely scolding preacher, whose aggression or exasperation only aggravates the pride it meets."[12]

8. Summarize Judah's future as depicted in chapter 14.

_____

_____

_____

9. What is the thrust of Jeremiah's prayer in 14:7-9, and in what ways could it serve as a model for our prayers as God's people today?

_____

_____

_____

_____

10. In 14:11-12, what is the significance of God's response to Jeremiah's prayer?

_____

_____

_____

Let my eyes overflow with tears night and day without ceasing (14:17). "For Jeremiah, the suffering of God's people was always an occasion for lamentation. . . . Jeremiah wept incessantly, the way a man would weep for his daughter if she had been wounded in war."[13]

For Further Study:
As God seeks to gain the people's attention in Jeremiah 13:15, he tells them, "Do not be arrogant." This command is also translated as "Do not be haughty" (NASB, NRSV) and "Be not proud" (ESV; NKJV: "Do not be proud"; NCV: "Don't be too proud"). How does pride block us from hearing God and from repentance? Let the following passages help you answer: 2 Kings 22:18-20; 2 Chronicles 12:5-8; 32:24-26; Luke 14:11; 18:14; James 4:6-10; 1 Peter 5:6-7.

For Thought and Discussion: From these chapters, what further impressions do you have of Jeremiah's personality and character?

Optional Application: On the basis of God's truth revealed in Jeremiah 11–14, perhaps the Holy Spirit has helped you sense a new and higher reality in your life that God is inviting you to. If this is true for you, express in your own words the reality that you long for, and use it as a springboard for prayer.

11. Summarize the exchange between Jeremiah and the Lord in 14:13-18, and what it reveals about both of them.

12. Jeremiah again questions God and prays on behalf of the people in 14:19-22. What does this reveal about Jeremiah's heart for the people?

13. What are the most important indicators of Jeremiah's reactions to God, as you see them in Jeremiah 11–14? Do you see them as a sign of Jeremiah's spiritual health? Why or why not?

14. What would you select as the key verse or passage in Jeremiah 11–14 — one that best captures or reflects the dynamics of what these chapters are all about?

15. List any lingering questions you have about Jeremiah 11–14.

For the Group

You may want to focus your discussion for lesson 3 especially on the following core biblical concepts, which are emphasized throughout Jeremiah.

- sin
- judgment
- repentance
- grace
- salvation

The following numbered questions in lesson 3 may stimulate your best and most helpful discussion: 1, 4, 9, 11, 13, 14, and 15.

Remember to look also at the "For Thought and Discussion" questions in the margins.

1. Derek Kidner, *The Message of Jeremiah*, The Bible Speaks Today (Downers Grove, IL: InterVarsity, 1987), 60.
2. Charles L. Feinberg, *Jeremiah*, The Expositor's Bible Commentary, vol. 6 (Grand Rapids, MI: Zondervan, 1986), 370–371.
3. Kidner, 60.
4. Feinberg, 456.
5. Philip Graham Ryken, *Jeremiah and Lamentations: From Sorrow to Hope*, Preaching the Word (Wheaton, IL: Crossway, 2001), 220.
6. Kidner, 61.
7. Ryken, 227, 231.
8. Feinberg, 461.
9. *NIV Study Bible* (Grand Rapids, MI: Zondervan, 1985), on Jeremiah 13:4.
10. Kidner, 63.
11. Ryken, 234.
12. Kidner, 64.
13. Ryken, 246.

JEREMIAH 15–20

Potter and Clay

1. Proverbs 2:1-5 tells about the sincere person who truly longs for wisdom and understanding, and who searches the Scriptures for it—as if there were treasure buried there. Such a person, this passage says, will come to understand the fear of the Lord and discover the knowledge of God. As you continue exploring Jeremiah, what "buried treasure" would you like God to help you find here—to show you what God and His wisdom are really like? If you have this desire, how would you express it in your own words of prayer to God?

_____

_____

_____

2. In one sitting if possible, read attentively through all of Jeremiah 15–20, taking notes and underlining or highlighting as you go. What impresses you overall as the key features and themes of this part of the book?

_____

_____

_____

3. From the previous lesson, recall Jeremiah's prayers in 14:7-9 and 14:20-22. What is therefore the significance of the Lord's reply in 15:1-9?

For Further Study:
Reflect on the spirit
of the Lord's lament
over Jerusalem in
15:5-9. How does it
compare with the
lament of Jesus in
Matthew 23:37-39?

"Chapter 14 ended with a powerful prayer on behalf of God's people. The prayer was flawless. Jeremiah made full confession for all the sins of the nation. He pleaded for God's mercy for the sake of God's glory. He affirmed that only God can answer prayer. It was the best of prayers, offered from the purest of motives. So God answered Jeremiah's prayer, right? Wrong. . . . Jeremiah's intercession proved to be a spectacular failure. In response, God promised to send judg-ment instead of blessing."[1]

Because of what Manasseh son of Hezekiah king of Judad did in Jerusalem (15:4, NRSV). See 2 Kings 21:1-16; 23:26; 24:3; 2 Chronicles 33:1-9.

---

4. In Jeremiah 15:10-18, what questions and concerns and emotions emerge in Jeremiah's mind and heart?

Jeremiah's "early ordeal, driving him to this desperate dialogue with God, was his baptism of fire. He emerged ready to stand his ground like a veteran, throughout the still fiercer sufferings of his final years."[2]

50

Lord, you understand; remember me and care for me (15:15). "Nothing is more revealing of a man of God than his prayer life. Jeremiah lived, worked, and wept in an atmosphere of prayer and openness before the Lord"; his prayers "are the most unreserved statements of any prophet in Israel. Other prophets narrate their experiences, but the Old Testament has few parallels to these self-disclosures. In them Jeremiah stands in all his human frailty, his love for his people, and his utter devotion to the will and call of God."[3]

For Further Study: Partaking of God's Word, Jeremiah found it to be "my joy and my heart's delight" (15:16). How does that relate to how God's Word is described in these passages: Psalms 19:10; 119:103; Proverbs 16:24; 24:13-14; Ezekiel 3:3?

"Most revealing of all . . . is his disappointment with his message, and consequently even with his Master, whose words were once a joy to him (15:16), but now a bitter pill. Whether he resented most the distastefulness of his predictions, or their seeming failure to materialize, or the persecution they provoked, we are not to know. What we do have is a reply (15:19-21) which (like the Lord's reply to Job) answered not the complaints but the complainer. That in itself was comment enough on where the trouble lay."[4]

Optional Application: How is Jeremiah's attitude toward God's word in Jeremiah 15:16 a model for our own approach to the Scriptures? How can his example be of practical help to us?

5. In Jeremiah 15:19-21, how would you summarize the Lord's reply to Jeremiah at this point?

_____

_____

_____

"In this amazing passage [15:19-21] Jeremiah recorded the Lord's greatest rebuke in the hour of his despair and his

For Thought and Discussion: We see many warnings in the book of Jeremiah. What is God warning His people about today?

hasty accusation of his Lord. . . . Jeremiah himself will have to undergo the refining process so that he can cleave to precious words, not vile, worthless ones."[5]

"Notice that there is no release from his calling: only a renewing of it."[6]

I am with you to rescue and save you (15:20). "The heartening promises of verses 20-21 remind Jeremiah of his opening call, almost word for word (see 1:18-19). They offer nothing easy. But the strength that they speak of, and the undefeated outcome, will be the glory of Jeremiah's maturity."[7] "This word of encouragement was sufficient for the prophet's need; and though opposition to his message mounted perilously, he never again complained to the Lord as he did in 15:10,15-18."[8]

---

6. Summarize everything that the Lord commands Jeremiah to do in 16:1-13, and the reasoning He gives for it.

_____

_____

_____

"It is one thing to grow eloquent over a dire prospect for a wicked nation; quite another thing to taste the medicine itself. To ask this of Jeremiah, denying him the cherished gift of wife and children (an almost unthinkable vocation at the time), and then to isolate him from sharing the occasions of sorrow and joy around him (16:5,8), was the measure of God's intense concern to get the message across."[9]

"Undoubtedly, the Lord's command for Jeremiah not to marry (16:2) was an emotional shock for him. Celibacy was unusual, not only in Israel, but throughout the Near East. Among the Jews marriage was viewed as man's natural state. . . . And now not only is he forbidden to marry, but he is also not allowed to participate in funerals (16:5) or times of joy (16:8). It was almost a sentence of social excommunication."[10]

"Jeremiah was a pariah, a misfit, a social outcast. . . . Jeremiah was a pariah because he was God's prophet. A prophet is a living sermon. Even his social life reveals something about the character and purposes of God. Jeremiah's refusal to participate in matrimony, sympathy, and revelry was a warning of the judgment to come."[11]

For Further Study: How does what God asked His prophet to do in Jeremiah 16 compare with what He asks from other prophets in Isaiah 20 and Ezekiel 24:15-24?

7. What are the promises God makes in Jeremiah 16:14-18 and 16:21, and what is their significance?

_____

_____

_____

8. In response to these promises, summarize Jeremiah's prophetic vision as stated in 16:19-20. What is the meaning and importance of this vision?

_____

_____

_____

For Further Study:
The Lord speaks in
Jeremiah 16:18 of a
double repayment for
the sins of His people.
How does this com-
pare with the words
of comfort from the
Lord given in Isaiah
40:1-2?

9. What is the significance of the way in which Judah's sin is characterized in 17:1-4?

_____

_____

_____

"Jeremiah's generation is beyond recall. The land is comprehensively defiled (17:2-3), and the people's heart has guilt not only written all over it but etched into it, engraved (verse 1) beyond erasure."[12]

10. How is the truth conveyed in Jeremiah 17:5-13 that all of us are answerable to God?

_____

_____

_____

Cursed is the one. . . . But blessed is the one . . . (17:5,7). "In God's book, the only alternative to cursed is blessed: there is no middle ground. The key to it here, as in the New Testament, is faith."[13]

The one who trusts in man. . . . The one who trusts in the Lord (17:5,7). "Everything will turn on where one's heart is."[14]

Cursed is the one . . . who draws strength from mere flesh (17:5). "This verse is a direct assault on American culture. It would be hard to imagine a statement that is more un-American, at least in the twenty-first century: 'Cursed is the one who trusts in man.' In other words, anyone who trusts in technology, economics, psychology, medicine, government, the military, the arts, or any other aspect of human culture is under God's curse. Yet these are exactly the things Americans trust for meaning and

54

security in life. American money says 'In God We Trust,' but what Americans really mean is 'In Self We Trust.'"[15]

Bear fruit (17:8). "This may or may not show in outward circumstances; it is the man himself (17:7-8) who is described, seen as heaven sees him."[16]

11. What is revealed about Jeremiah's heart in his prayer of deliverance in 17:14-18?

_____

_____

_____

12. How would you summarize the point of the Lord's message to His people in 17:19-27?

_____

_____

_____

_____

Keep the Sabbath day holy (17:22). "Sabbath-keeping was explicitly a badge of loyalty, a sign of the covenant with the Lord (Exodus 31:12-17). It was a good criterion. A people's or a person's reaction to the gift of a day to be set apart for God was a fair indicator of their spiritual temperature; and it still is."[17]

13. In chapter 18, what appeal is God making to His people through the parable of the potter and the clay?

_____

_____

_____

For Further Study: Reflect on Jeremiah's request for healing in Jeremiah 17:14. With this picture in mind, describe the importance given to God's healing in the following passages: Exodus 15:22-26; 2 Kings 2:19-22; Psalm 147:3; Isaiah 57:18-19; Ezekiel 47:12; Hosea 14:4; Luke 4:18; 1 Peter 2:24; Revelation 22:2.

Optional Application: In what ways is Jeremiah's prayer for healing in Jeremiah 17:14 a reflection of your own heart and need at this time?

For Further Study: How does the message about the Sabbath in Jeremiah 17:19-27 compare with what you see in Nehemiah 13:15-22 and Isaiah 58:13-14?

For Further Study:
"The potter at work is one of God's favorite pictures of himself."[18] Summarize the meaning of this picture as you see it used in Psalm 119:73; Isaiah 29:15-16; 45:9; 64:8; and Romans 9:20-24.

Then I will relent and not inflict . . . the disaster I had planned (18:8). "This is a statement of first-class importance for our understanding of all prophecy, removing it entirely from the realm of fatalism."[19]

In chapter 18 "we have a true but mysterious blending of the divine sovereignty and human responsibility."[20] "The doctrinal point of this passage can be stated very simply: God can do whatever he wants with you. This is what it means for him to be God. Because God is God, he is free to do whatever he pleases. In his hands rest all power, rule, control, authority, kingdom, government, and dominion."[21]

Listen to me, LORD (18:19). "Characteristically, Jeremiah pours out his heart in yet another of the anguished protests which punctuate these chapters and illuminate his story. His wound would have hurt less had he cared less and, paradoxically, prayed less for his people; but the violent swing from love to hate shows how near the surface are the unruly instincts of the best of us."[22]

Give their children over to famine. . . . Do not forgive their crimes (18:21,23). "The prayer of verse 23 against forgiveness needs to be read in Old Testament terms, of punishment in this world rather than the next, and of judicial sentencing. Yet granted all this, the gulf between praying down famine on even the adversaries' children and praying down forgiveness on one's tormentors is the gulf between the resentful 'lamb led to the slaughter' (as Jeremiah described himself, 11:19) and the uncomplaining Lamb of God."[23]

14. What is the point of the story of the broken flask in chapter 19?

_____

_____

_____

_____

"Jeremiah 18 was an object lesson in God's sovereignty. Jeremiah 19 is an even more dramatic lesson in God's wrath."[24]

I will make them eat the flesh of their sons and daughters (19:9). See the fulfillment of this as recalled in the eyewitness account of Lamentations 4:10.

Break the jar while those who go with you are watching (19:10). "Jeremiah was to make his oracle unforgettable (and irreversible, as an acted word from the Lord), by smashing the clay pot as something that was now past remaking. Then, with great courage, he made his way to the stronghold of his enemies, the temple court, with the dire results that will occupy the next chapter."[25]

"Escaping the wrath of God may not be a 'felt need' for many people, but it is most certainly a real need. . . . The wrath of God is just and fearsome, but not inevitable. Jesus Christ provides the way— the only way—to escape the wrath of God."[26]

15. Summarize what happens in Jeremiah 20 and how the Lord and Jeremiah both respond to this.

_____

_____

_____

_____

57

For Thought and Discussion: Chapter 20 has been called Jeremiah's "dark night of the soul." In what ways do you see this as indeed being his experience here? In what ways can you relate to what he was going through?

For Further Study: As you reflect on the dramatic swing in Jeremiah's thoughts between verses 13 and 14 in chapter 20, observe similar swings in Job's thoughts as detected by comparing Job 2:10 with 3:1-10, and 19:25-27 with 21:5-6.

For Thought and Discussion: From these chapters, what further impressions do you have of Jeremiah's personality and character?

"Jeremiah 20 is best understood as the prophet's account of his night in the stocks, his dark night of the soul."[27]

Put in the stocks (20:2). "The Hebrew word is formed from the verb to twist, implying that this 'twist-frame' clamped the victim in a position that would become increasingly distressing."[28]

The LORD is with me. . . . He rescues the life of the needy from the hands of the wicked (20:11,13). "He emerges from his doubts—and surely in verse 13 we have his very words as he emerges also from his overnight confinement (the needy is in the singular)."[29]

Cursed be the day I was born! (20:14). "Like Job, plunging to the depths after each high point of faith, Jeremiah suffers a desolating reaction which brings now the long series of his protests and laments to a close. After this, he goes on to his worst ordeals with never a hesitation or a word of doubt. . . . What these curses convey, therefore, is a state of mind, not a prosaic plea. The heightened language is not there to be analyzed; it is there to bowl us over. Together with other tortured cries from him and his fellow sufferers, these raw wounds in Scripture remain lest we forget the sharpness of the age-long struggle, or the frailty of the finest overcomers."[30] "Sudden transitions are frequent in Jeremiah"; in that of Jeremiah 20:14-15, "the transition and contrast are psychologically understandable in view of the constant pressures on Jeremiah. Feeling an utter failure after being in the stocks, he wished he had never been born. The passage is emotionally authentic because he was being prepared for the greatest blow of all—the destruction of the beloved city of Jerusalem. The experience of Jeremiah at this time shows how difficult the task of God's servants can be and how readily available the grace of God is to sustain them in their darkest hours."[31]

---

16. What would you select as the key verse or passage in Jeremiah 15–20 — one that best captures or reflects the dynamics of what these chapters are all about?

_____

_____

_____

17. List any lingering questions you have about Jeremiah 15–20.

_____

_____

_____

_____

Optional Application: On the basis of God's truth revealed in Jeremiah 15–20, perhaps the Holy Spirit has helped you sense a new and higher reality in your life that God is inviting you to. If this is true for you, express in your own words the reality that you long for, and use it as a springboard for prayer.

For the Group

You may want to focus your discussion for lesson 4 especially on the following core biblical concepts, which are emphasized throughout Jeremiah.

- sin
- judgment
- repentance
- grace
- salvation

The following numbered questions in lesson 4 may stimulate your best and most helpful discussion: 2, 7, 11, 12, 13, 16, and 17.

Remember to look also at the "For Thought and Discussion" questions in the margins.

1. Philip Graham Ryken, _Jeremiah and Lamentations: From Sorrow to Hope_, Preaching the Word (Wheaton, IL: Crossway, 2001), 254.
2. Derek Kidner, _The Message of Jeremiah_, The Bible Speaks Today (Downers Grove, IL: InterVarsity, 1987), 17.
3. Charles L. Feinberg, _Jeremiah_, The Expositor's Bible Commentary, vol. 6 (Grand Rapids, MI: Zondervan, 1986), 371.
4. Kidner, 69.
5. Feinberg, 477.

6. Kidner, 69.
7. Kidner, 70.
8. Feinberg, 478.
9. Kidner, 70.
10. Feinberg, 479.
11. Ryken, 263–264.
12. Kidner, 71.
13. Kidner, 72.
14. Kidner, 72.
15. Ryken, 274.
16. Kidner, 73.
17. Kidner, 74.
18. Kidner, 76.
19. Kidner, 76.
20. Feinberg, 490.
21. Ryken, 294.
22. Kidner, 78.
23. Kidner, 78.
24. Ryken, 304.
25. Kidner, 79.
26. Ryken, 309–310.
27. Ryken, 315.
28. Kidner, 79.
29. Kidner, 80.
30. Kidner, 81.
31. Feinberg, 504.

JEREMIAH 21–24

Prophecies Against Judah

1. In one sitting if possible, read all of Jeremiah 21–24, taking notes and underlining or highlighting as you go. What impresses you overall as the key features and themes of this part of the book?

_____

_____

_____

"The book of Jeremiah is prophecy, not chronicle, therefore many of the following chapters move freely back and forth within these final years, as their datelines show."[1]

2. Summarize the Lord's message to Zedekiah and to the house of David as you see it developed in chapter 21.

_____

_____

_____

For Thought and Discussion: What are the most important leadership lessons that you're seeing in the book of Jeremiah, especially in these middle chapters of the book?

For Further Study: As you reflect on the Lord's warnings to King Zedekiah in Jeremiah 21, note also the other events, visions, and prophecies from the Lord that occurred during this king's reign, as mentioned in Jeremiah 24:8-10; 27–28; 32:1-5; 34; 37–39; 49:34; 51:59; 52.

King Zedekiah (21:1). Reigned in Judah from 597 to 586 BC. He was installed as king by the Babylonian invaders who took captive the previous king, Jehoiachin (also called Jeconiah and Coniah). "This signified no improvement in the quality of . . . leadership. Although he seems not to have been personally hostile to Jeremiah, Zedekiah was completely under the sway of his pro-Egyptian advisers, who continually plotted evil against Jeremiah and urged rebellion against Babylon (e.g., 28:1-4). Jeremiah insisted that the only sane course was submission to Babylon, but for this counsel he was branded unpatriotic and apprehended as a traitor."[2]

Nebuchadnezzar king of Babylon is attacking us (21:2). "This episode, c. 588, transports us suddenly to the final siege of Jerusalem, some twenty years after the events of chapter 20. For its context, we must wait for chapters 32, 34, 37–39."[3]

"Once more Jeremiah gives us a cluster of prophecies (chapters 22–23) linked not by chronology but by similar themes."[4]

3. Summarize the Lord's message to Judah's king as you observe it in 22:1-9.

_____

_____

_____

_____

4. Summarize the Lord's message to Shallum (Jehoahaz) in 22:10-12.

_____

_____

_____

_____

What the LORD says about Shallum son of Josiah, who succeeded his father as king of Judah (22:11). Shallum is also called Jehoahaz; his reign is described in 2 Kings 23:31-33. "After a short rule of three months he was summarily deposed by Pharaoh Neco (then master of Palestine) and deported to Egypt. The first leader of Judah to die in exile, Jehoahaz received the announcement of his judgment from Jeremiah (22:10-12)."[5]

5. Summarize the Lord's message to Jehoiakim in 22:13-23.

_____

_____

_____

_____

What the LORD says about Jehoiakim son of Josiah king of Judah (22:18). Egypt's Pharaoh Neco placed Jehoiakim on the throne in place of his deposed brother Shallum (Jehoahaz). "This was an unhappy choice, both for the nation and for Jeremiah. Jehoiakim was not inclined to follow the godly example of his father Josiah, but reverted to idolatry, self-indulgence, and rebellion. Surrounded by a circle of ambitious nobles and self-appointed prophets, Jehoiakim and his party lived under the illusion that their future was guaranteed by the presence of the Solomonic temple in their midst and by eternal divine favor to David's royal lineage. Their corrupt behavior and false sense of security elicited the most vigorous protests from Jeremiah."[6]

6. Summarize the Lord's message to Coniah (also called Jeconiah or Jehoiachin) in 22:24-30.

_____

_____

For Further Study:
Jehoiakim's father, King Josiah, is commended in Jeremiah 22:15-16 for his commitment to justice, righteousness, and compassion for the needy. How do you see these themes further taught in Isaiah 58:6-12?

For Further Study:
As you reflect on the Lord's warnings to King Jehoiakim in Jeremiah 22:13-23, note also the other events, visions, and prophecies from the Lord that occurred during this king's reign, as mentioned in Jeremiah 24:1; 25:1; 26:1,21-23; 35:1; 36:1,9,27-32; 45:1; 46:2.

For Further Study:
How does Jeremiah
23:1-8 compare with
God's words about
shepherds in Ezekiel
34?

**For Thought and
Discussion:** How
are these chapters
communicating how
highly God values our
truthfulness? Why is
this so important to
God?

**Optional
Application:** In
your own leadership
responsibilities, what
lessons are you learn-
ing from the book of
Jeremiah, especially
from these middle
chapters? In what
ways do these chap-
ters relate to how you
lead or guide or influ-
ence others?

**Optional
Application:** What
do you find to per-
sonally praise our
Lord Jesus for in the
messianic prophecy
of 23:5-6? What do
these truths mean
in your own under-
standing of Christ and
your relationship with
Him?

*I will hurl you . . . into another country . . . and
there you both will die* (22:26). See the fulfillment of this in 2 Kings 24:10-16 and Jeremiah
24:1. He was later treated well in his captivity;
see 2 Kings 25:27-30 and Jeremiah 52:31-34.

7. What does 23:1-8 indicate about God's perspective on leadership among His people? What does
He look for in leaders?

*I myself will gather the remnant of my flock . . .
and will bring them back to their pasture*
(23:3). "God promises to shepherd the lost
sheep of Israel. He wants the job done right; so
he promises to do it himself."[7]

8. What's most important for us to see in the messianic prophecy of 23:5-6?

9. What are the greatest contrasts you see
between the description of Judah's kings given
in chapters 21 and 22 and the description of
"the Righteous Branch" here in 23:5-6?

The Lᴏʀᴅ Our Righteousness (23:6). This name for Messiah is also the name given in 33:16 to Jerusalem in her promised future. The messianic name "speaks of one who will not only reflect the righteousness of God but will convey it to his people, making it their own possession."[8]

10. Jeremiah 23:7-8 repeats the words of 16:14-15. The repetition highlights the importance of this promise. What particular significance do you see in these words?

_____

_____

_____

11. What does 23:9-40 emphasize regarding God's perspective on prophecy among His people? What does He look for in prophets and in all those who proclaim and teach His Word?

_____

_____

_____

Which of them has stood in the council of the Lᴏʀᴅ to see or to hear his word? (23:18). "In verses 18-22 we reach the heart of the matter: God is speaking of the difference between conjecture and revelation."[9] "Jeremiah . . . showed clearly that no prophet of God can ever derive his message from observing the times he lives in."[10]

If they had stood in my council, they would have proclaimed my words to my people and would have turned them from their evil ways (23:22). "If they had been in the intimate circle where God divulges his plans to his faithful followers . . . they would have uttered God's truth to his needy people. The result would have been the repentance of the nation and

For Further Study:
Consider again the imagery used and the promises conveyed in Jeremiah 23:5-6. What connection is there with the messianic implications you find in these passages: Isaiah 11:1; Jeremiah 33:14-16; Ezekiel 17:22-24; Zechariah 3:8; 6:12-13? Also, how does the name "The Lᴏʀᴅ Our Righteousness" in Jeremiah 23:6 connect with the truths you see in Romans 3:21-26 and 1 Corinthians 1:30-31?

For Further Study:
Keeping in mind the Lord's confrontation with false prophets in Jeremiah 23:16-22, what standards and guidelines for His prophets do you see in Deuteronomy 13:1-11 and 18:15-22? Also, compare what Jeremiah 23 records about the deceptive foolishness of the prophets with what you see in Jeremiah 29:8-9 and Ezekiel 13.

their restoration to godliness. A proof of the true prophet was his desire to win others to the way of godliness in which he himself was walking. The results of his ministry were indicators of the genuineness of his call and message."[11]

Is not my word like fire . . . and like a hammer that breaks a rock in pieces? (23:29). "God's truth is like fire in contrast to the useless, powerless words of the false prophets. It is penetrating, purifying, and consumes evil. Jeremiah himself had experienced this (see 5:14; 20:9). Moreover, God's word is full of power like a hammer strongly wielded (see Hebrews 4:12-13). His message does not lull men in their sins; it crushes the heart to bring it to repentance. The true word convicts and converts; it neither amuses nor entertains."[12]

12. What is the point of the story of the good and bad fruit in chapter 24?

_____

_____

_____

_____

13. What significance do you see in the promise God makes in 24:6-7? In particular, how does it demonstrate God's grace?

_____

_____

_____

14. What would you select as the key verse or passage in Jeremiah 21–24 — one that best captures or reflects the dynamics of what these chapters are all about?

_____

_____

_____

15. List any lingering questions you have about
    Jeremiah 21–24.

_____

_____

_____

For the Group

You may want to focus your discussion for lesson 5
especially on the following core biblical concepts,
which are emphasized throughout Jeremiah.

- sin
- judgment
- repentance
- grace
- salvation

The following numbered questions in lesson 5
may stimulate your best and most helpful discussion: 1, 7, 8, 10, 11, 13, 14, and 15.

Remember to look also at the "For Thought and
Discussion" questions in the margins.

1. Derek Kidner, *The Message of Jeremiah*, The Bible Speaks
   Today (Downers Grove, IL: InterVarsity, 1987), 83.
2. Geoffrey W. Bromiley, ed., *International Standard Bible
   Encyclopedia*, vol. 2 (Grand Rapids, MI: Eerdmans, 1982),
   986.
3. Kidner, 84.
4. Charles L. Feinberg, *Jeremiah*, The Expositor's Bible Commentary, vol. 6 (Grand Rapids, MI: Zondervan, 1986), 510.
5. Bromiley, 985.
6. Bromiley, 985.
7. Philip Graham Ryken, *Jeremiah and Lamentations: From
   Sorrow to Hope*, Preaching the Word (Wheaton, IL: Crossway, 2001), 337.
8. Kidner, 90.
9. Kidner, 91.
10. Feinberg, 523.
11. Feinberg, 523.
12. Feinberg, 524–525.

JEREMIAH 25–29
The Cup of His Wrath

"After the preview given in chapters 21–24 of the disastrous years 609–597, in which no fewer than four kings came to the throne after the death of Josiah, we return to the moment when the second of these kings, Jehoiakim, found himself the subject of a new world-ruler, Nebuchadrezzar of Babylon.... It was a time that raised alarming questions over the rise and fall of empires and the future of one's own people."[1]

1. In one sitting if possible, read attentively through all of Jeremiah 25–29, taking notes and underlining or highlighting as you go. What impresses you overall as the key features and themes of this part of the book?

_____

_____

_____

For Thought and Discussion: From what you've seen so far in Jeremiah, what observations can you offer about the process of spiritual decline? What dangers do we need to be alert to in this regard?

In the fourth year of Jehoiakim . . . which was the first year of Nebuchadnezzar king of

Babylon (25:1). "In the critical fourth year of Jehoiakim's reign, 605 B.C., the armies of Babylon under the leadership of Nebuchadrezzar [Nebuchadnezzar] defeated the forces of Pharaoh Neco at Carchemish, and thus gained control of the upper Euphrates and Syro-Palestine (Jeremiah 46:2). Jeremiah clearly foresaw the course of events from there: Nebuchadrezzar would advance into Palestine, take Judah captive, and send the people into exile for seventy years (25:1-14). It was in that year, too, that Jeremiah was commissioned to write his oracles on a scroll which was later burned by the king. In reply, Jeremiah uttered a prophetic judgment concerning Jehoiakim's ignominious death and proceeded to dictate a second scroll (chapter 36)."[2]

Chapter 25 "deals with a time of national and international ramifications.... Not only is chapter 25 important historically, geographically, and prophetically, it is also remarkable for the abundance of its ideas, the variety of its figures, and the diversity of its style in treating the same theme of sin, repentance, and judgment. It is without parallel in world literature."[3]

2. Summarize the major points of Jeremiah's message in 25:3-14.

_____

_____

_____

The LORD has sent all his servants the prophets to you again and again (25:4). "God understands the value of repetition. In the Bible he repeatedly warns his people about the things he hates. This is part of God's grace. He does not keep people guessing about how to please him. He gives his instructions over and over again."[4]

Seventy years (25:11). This "turned out to be a round number which God mercifully shortened; for Babylon fell to Cyrus not in 535 but four years earlier, in 539."[5] Seventy years was considered a normal life-span (see Psalm 90:10; Isaiah 23:15).

3. Compare the prophecy you see in Jeremiah 25:11-14 with what is promised later in 29:10; 32:36-38; and 33:7-13. What is the overall message of these passages? And why is this message so important for Israel to grasp?

_____

_____

_____

4. Summarize the message that Jeremiah is given for all the world in 25:15-38.

_____

_____

_____

They will stagger and go mad (25:16). "The horrors of war will drive the nations mad."[6]

All the kingdoms on the face of the earth (25:26). Recall the international scope in Jeremiah's initial calling—when God told him, "I appointed you as a prophet to the nations" and "I appoint you over nations and kingdoms" (Jeremiah 1:5,10).

5. Back in chapter 7 we were given a longer version (or an earlier instance) of the sermon we now see in 26:1-6. What reactions to Jeremiah's message are emphasized in chapter 26?

_____

_____

_____

71

"Here in chapter 26 the emphasis is on the results of the temple address and on a brief summary of it. In a sense, the first verses of this chapter give us a condensation of chapters 7–10. The heart of the temple address was that unless Judah repented, Jerusalem would be as Shiloh. By his specific warnings, Jeremiah had incurred the wrath of the false prophets and their followers. And later on when he predicted the seventy years' captivity, they tried to bring about his death."[7]

I will make this house like Shiloh (26:6). See 7:12-15 and Psalm 78:60.

Zion will be plowed like a field (26:18). See Micah 3:12.

Did not the Lord relent, so that he did not bring the disaster he pronounced against them? (26:19). See 2 Kings 18–19 and Isaiah 37.

---

6. What significance do you see in the story told in Jeremiah 26:20-24?

_____

_____

_____

Ahikam son of Shaphan supported Jeremiah (26:24). Members of Shaphan's family were among those who "had stood by Jeremiah in his darkest years" and "steadily took the lead in befriending him"[8] See also 36:10-11,25; 40:5-6.

"Chapters 27–28 attack the false optimism

of the prophets of Judah . . . [and] dispel the erroneous view that Babylon was just a passing power, not to be reckoned with."[9]

For Further Study: How do you see the prophecy in Jeremiah 27:21-22 being fulfilled in Ezra 1:7-8 and 5:13-17?

7. Summarize the major points the Lord communicates about Nebuchadnezzar in chapter 27.

_____

_____

_____

For Thought and Discussion: How do you see Jeremiah's life as an example of faithfulness in ministry and faithfulness to the Lord during hard times? What particular lessons does his life demonstrate in this regard?

8. What does chapter 27 communicate most regarding God's sovereignty?

_____

_____

_____

9. How would you contrast the prophets Hananiah and Jeremiah, as we see them both presented in chapter 28?

_____

_____

_____

This is what the LORD Almighty, the God of Israel, says (28:2). "Hananiah had the temerity to use the same introductory formula as Jeremiah, implying a claim for inspiration similar to his."[10]

Amen! May the LORD do so! May the LORD fulfill the words you have prophesied by bringing . . . all the exiles back to this place from Babylon (28:6). "His prayer must have come from the heart. He truly wished that Hananiah's prophecy would come true, that the Exile would end within two years."[11]

Optional Application: In the church today, should we be on our guard against false prophets like Hananiah? If so, what should we be alert to? What should we guard against? What should we be watching for?

For Thought and Discussion: Jeremiah's letter in chapter 29 has been called a "letter of hope." Why is hope so important for us, and for all of God's people? Is there ever a time when we don't need it?

10. From 29:1-9, summarize the instructions from the Lord that Jeremiah includes in his letter to those who were earlier taken captive to Babylon.

_____

_____

_____

_____

In chapter 29 "we have the first letter [chronologically] recorded in the Bible. (For other Old Testament letters, see 2 Chronicles 21:12-15; 30:1,6-9; 32:17; Ezra 1:2-4; 4:9-22; 5:7-16; 6:3-12; 7:12-26.) The historical situation of the chapter was that in 597 B.C., some three thousand Jews had been exiled with Jehoiachin, among them a number of priests and prophets along with the royal household. In Jerusalem, Jeremiah heard that some exiled false prophets were predicting an early fall of Babylon and an early restoration of the exiles to Judah. Jeremiah's letters warned the exiles against this deception and urged them to wait patiently for God's time."[12]

Seek the peace and prosperity of the city to which I have carried you into exile. Pray to the LORD for it, because if it prospers, you too will prosper (29:7). "What emerges in the call to them . . . is gloriously positive: a liberation from the paralyzing sullenness of inertia and self-pity, into doing, for a start, what comes to hand and makes for growth, but above all what makes for peace. To set themselves something to live for, and something to give their captors, through their enterprise and their intercession, was incidentally the surest way—and still is—to the givers' own enrichment."[13]

---

11. Summarize the promises God gives to these captives in 29:10-14.

_____

_____

_____

I will come to you and fulfill my good promise to bring you back (29:10). Recall the promise seen earlier in 25:11-14.

_____

12. How does 29:10-14 especially emphasize God's grace?

_____

_____

_____

_____

13. Summarize the warning about false prophets as given in 29:15-23.

_____

_____

_____

You may say, "The Lord has raised up prophets for us in Babylon" (29:15). "Among the captives as well as in Jerusalem, there were prophets stirring up false hopes of almost instant freedom."[14]

14. Describe the falsehood that is exposed in 29:24-32.

_____

_____

_____

Optional Application: To what degree, and in what ways, might the instructions and promises given to God's people in 29:1-14 be applicable to Christians today as we live in the midst of a secular culture and world?

For Further Study: What does it mean to seek God with one's whole heart, as God requests His people to do in Jeremiah 29:13? Allow these passages to help you form an answer: Leviticus 26:40-42; Deuteronomy 4:29-31; 30:1-6; Psalm 119:1-3,9-11,145-149; Isaiah 55:6-7; Hosea 6:1-3; Joel 2:12-13; Luke 11:9-10; James 4:7-10.

Optional Application: In Jeremiah 29:11, God declares to His people, "For I know the plans I have for you ... plans to prosper you and not to harm you, plans to give you hope and a future." To what degree is this a personal affirmation to you from God? What is your essential expectation in regard to your own future, and God's plans for it?

15. What would you select as the key verse or passage in Jeremiah 25–29 — one that best captures or reflects the dynamics of what these chapters are all about?

_____

_____

_____

16. List any lingering questions you have about Jeremiah 25–29.

_____

_____

_____

For the Group

You may want to focus your discussion for lesson 6 especially on the following core biblical concepts, which are emphasized throughout Jeremiah.

- sin
- judgment
- repentance
- grace
- salvation

The following numbered questions in lesson 6 may stimulate your best and most helpful discussion: 1, 4, 8, 11, 12, 15, and 16.

Once more, look also at the questions in the margins under the heading "For Thought and Discussion."

1. Derek Kidner, *The Message of Jeremiah*, The Bible Speaks Today (Downers Grove, IL: InterVarsity, 1987), 94.
2. Geoffrey W. Bromiley, ed., *International Standard Bible Encyclopedia*, vol. 2 (Grand Rapids, MI: Eerdmans, 1982), 985.

3. Charles L. Feinberg, *Jeremiah*, The Expositor's Bible Commentary, vol. 6 (Grand Rapids, MI: Zondervan, 1986), 530.
4. Philip Graham Ryken, *Jeremiah and Lamentations: From Sorrow to Hope*, Preaching the Word (Wheaton, IL: Crossway, 2001), 359.
5. Kidner, 95.
6. Feinberg, 533.
7. Feinberg, 537.
8. Kidner, 21.
9. Feinberg, 543.
10. Feinberg, 547–548.
11. Ryken, 400.
12. Feinberg, 551–552.
13. Kidner, 100.
14. Kidner, 100.

JEREMIAH 30–33

From Sorrow to Hope

Chapters 30–33 have been called Jeremiah's "Book of Consolation." "Though written during a time of deep distress for Jerusalem, they foretell a glorious future for the nation. . . . Jeremiah is occupied not with the near future but with the distant consummation of Israel's history. He was in prison, the city in dire straits by famine and disease; yet it was then that he spoke words of greatest comfort. He predicted the permanence of the nation, the coming of the Gentiles to the truth, the institution of God's new covenant of redemption, and the rule of the Davidic King over cleansed Zion. These chapters amply refute the superficial charge that Jeremiah was only a pessimist."[1]

"Even Isaiah rises to no greater heights of delighted eloquence than does Jeremiah in these chapters. . . . Surpassing even the prospect of return and reunion, there emerges the promise of a new covenant, in which the Old Testament itself would be transcended by the New. . . .

"Throughout this God-given dream of things to come, the language and the landscape are those of Jeremiah's day, dominated by the theme of exile and restoration. Nevertheless a vaster ingathering than the modest one of 538 is foretold. . . . And the covenant with Israel and Judah would, in the event, embrace the world-wide 'children of the living God' (Romans 9:26). . . . Even the rebuilding of the city is envisaged in terms which outstrip the literal event, to draw the mind beyond the 'Jerusalem which now is' to 'Jerusalem that is above' (Galatians 4:25-26).

"So, as elsewhere in prophecy, God had both an immediate and a distant prospect to unfold, using language which spoke to the prophet's generation

For Thought and Discussion: Would you describe the message of Jeremiah (in all that you've studied so far) as being mostly negative or mostly positive?

in the first place, but which pointed by its very exuberance to a greater fulfillment on a different plane: a secret 'hidden for ages and generations' (Colossians 1:26), to be revealed only when its time arrived."[2] In the latter days, says God to His people in this very prophecy, you will understand this (see Jeremiah 30:24).

1. In one sitting if possible, read attentively through all of Jeremiah 30–33, taking notes and underlining or highlighting as you go. What impresses you overall as the key features and themes of these chapters?

2. Summarize and outline the many promises given to God's people in chapter 30.

3. What does chapter 30 communicate about the character of God?

They will serve the L*ord *their God and David their king, whom I will raise up for them (30:9). "The promise . . . would have to wait for the coming—indeed the coming in glory—of David's Lord. So at once we have a prophecy that looks far beyond the middle distance to the last days."[3]

I will not completely destroy you (30:11). Recall this crucial promise given earlier in Jeremiah 5:10,18.

***Your wound is incurable, your injury beyond
    healing*** (30:12). "Liberation is a costly busi-
ness: its other face is judgment, and the people
to be liberated need saving from themselves
as much as from their enemies. Such are the
somber realities that prepare for the radiance of
chapter 31."[4]

***Their leader will be one of their own; their ruler
    will arise from among them. I will bring him
    near and he will come close to me*** (30:21).
"Embedded in this passage [30:21-22] so full
of promise is one of the most beautiful of the
messianic predictions in the Old Testament.
First . . . the coming ruler . . . will come from
native soil (see Zechariah 6:12). Second, he will
have the privilege of approach to God. Usage
of the Old Testament shows that this means
priestly position and ministry (see Psalm 110:4;
Zechariah 6:13). The verbs convey this. The
ruler will need no mediator. Thus he will be
greater than even David and Solomon. Like
Melchizedek he will have a dual role."[5]

So you will be my people, and I will be your God
    (30:22; see also 31:33). This "quiet couplet . . .
with the radical simplicity of a marriage vow,
has always expressed the heart of God's covenant, from Genesis to Revelation."[6] "Jeremiah
turns to the result of Messiah's ministry: the
old covenant is renewed."[7]

***The storm of the LORD . . . swirling down on
    the heads of the wicked*** (30:23). "Evil will
not simply disappear; it must be punished and
destroyed."[8]

---

4. Summarize and outline the promises God gives
   to His people in 31:1-30.

_____

_____

_____

_____

For Further Study:
In the following
passages, observe
how the state-
ment in Jeremiah
30:22 is emphasized
throughout Scripture:
Genesis 17:7; Exodus
6:7; Leviticus 26:12;
Jeremiah 31:33;
Ezekiel 11:19-20;
Hosea 2:19-23;
Zechariah 13:9;
Hebrews 8:10;
Revelation 21:3,7.

For Further Study:
Explore the Father's
"everlasting love"
(Jeremiah 31:3) in
these passages:
Deuteronomy 7:7-9;
Psalm 103:17; Isaiah
45:17; 54:8-9; Hosea
2:19-20; Romans 8:38-
39; Ephesians 1:3-6;
2 Timothy 1:9.

I have loved you with an everlasting love (31:3).
This "great saying" represents "the fountain-head of the whole passage and of the whole chapter . . . for it is this, not any merit in the beloved, that has begun and will carry forward the relationship, through thick and thin, to its perfection."[9]

5. What is especially emphasized about God's character in 31:1-30?

_____

_____

_____

_____

Ramah (31:15). "Ramah was a town five miles north of Jerusalem, the very place where exiles were gathered before deportation to Babylon (see 40:1). . . . Jeremiah himself was in a camp for exiles in Ramah (40:1)."[10]

Rachel weeping for her children (31:15). "The focus . . . is on the grief of the exile, as if it touched Rachel herself."[11] "She who had so longed for children (see Genesis 30:1) is cruelly bereaved of them, but God purposes to restore them."[12] In the New Testament, Matthew applies this verse to Herod's slaughter of infants in Bethlehem after the birth of Jesus (see Matthew 2:18).

A new covenant (31:31). "A Biblical covenant is a binding relationship of eternal consequence in which God promises to bless and his people promise to obey."[13]

6. What is the "new covenant," as you see it taught in 31:31-40?

_____

_____

For Further Study:
How would you compare Jeremiah 31:27-30 with what the Lord declares through another prophet in Ezekiel 18:1-4?

For Thought and Discussion: What is your current understanding of the phrase "new covenant," and what it means in biblical doctrine?

A thematic outline of 31:31-40 —
"1. The time of the covenant (verse 31) . . .
"2. The Maker of the covenant (verse 31) . . .
"3. The name of the covenant (verse 31) . . .
"4. The parties of the covenant (verse 31) . . .
"5. The contrasted covenant (verse 32)—not like the old covenant . . .
"6. The nature of the covenant (verses 32-34) — not dependent on external law nor human interpretation . . .
"7. The immutability of the covenant (verses 35-37) — the unchanging purpose of God reflected in the fixed order of nature.
"8. The physical aspects of the covenant (verses 38-40) — rebuilt Jerusalem in holiness and permanence.
"9. The Guarantor of the covenant (verses 31-40) — 'declares the Lord' or 'the Lord says' (nine times), as though to swear by himself (see Hebrews 6:17-18)."[14]

I will make a new covenant (31:31). "The old covenant had taken a new lease of life in Jeremiah's early days, when the lost 'book of the covenant' (2 Chronicles 34:30) was found and read and reaffirmed, to become the blueprint of Josiah's continuing reformation. Yet everything that we have read in Jeremiah confirms that 'the law made nothing perfect' (Hebrews 7:19), for the response was skin-deep, and died with the death of Josiah. This, then, was God's moment to speak of a covenant that would be heart-deep and everlasting (see not only 31:33-34 but 32:40). As with all God's covenants, it would come of his initiative, not ours."[15] "This mountain-peak Old Testament passage stands in a real sense as the climax of Jeremiah's teaching. Every one of its phrases and clauses is vital."[16]

83

For Further Study:
Compare the prom-
ises in Jeremiah
31:31-34 with
what you see in
Deuteronomy 30:6;
Jeremiah 32:39-41;
Ezekiel 11:17-20;
Joel 2:28-29; and
Zechariah 7:12. Also,
how is this concept
of the new covenant
expanded and inten-
sified in chapters
8–10 of Hebrews?
(See also Matthew
26:26-29; Luke 22:20;
Hebrews 12:24.)

**Optional
Application:**
Keeping in mind the
promise in Jeremiah
31:40 of an inde-
structible, immov-
able city for God's
people, reflect as
well on these words:
"Therefore, since
we are receiving a
kingdom that can-
not be shaken, let us
be thankful, and so
worship God accept-
ably with reverence
and awe" (Hebrews
12:28). With your full-
est understanding
of what this means
personally for you,
offer gratitude and
worship to God.

How does the New Covenant apply to God's
people in all ages? "The same death of Christ
that implemented the new covenant for Israel
does so for all sinners for all time. The testimony of the entire New Testament is too clear
on this point to be misunderstood. Because
Israel rejected the covenant in the first advent,
Gentiles availed themselves of its provisions (see
Romans 9:30-33); and Israel will yet ratify it at the
climax of her history (see Zechariah 12:10–13:1).
Thus it is correct to say that all believers in Christ
are by virtue of this covenant grafted into the
stock of Abraham (see Romans 11:16-24)."[17]

*The city will never again be uprooted or demol-
ished* (31:40). This promise "is a further sign
that we must look beyond 'the present Jerusalem' to 'the Jerusalem above' (Galatians
4:25-26): the great company of saints and
angels which is already our home city, as seen
in, for example, Hebrews 12:22-24; Revelation
21:1–22:5."[18]

*In the tenth year of Zedekiah king of Judah,
which was the eighteenth year of Nebuchadnezzar* (32:1). "We are now projected into the
year 588/7, only months before the fall of a
starving and plague-ridden Jerusalem (32:24),
and with Jeremiah now in prison (32:2; 33:1).
What has led up to this will be told in subse-
quent chapters; but these two [Jeremiah 32–33]
are placed here no doubt to reinforce the buoy-
ant prophecies of chapters 30–31, by showing
in sober prose how unpromising, humanly
speaking, were the conditions in which such
words from God were spoken, and with what
conviction they were stood by."[19]

7. Describe what actions Jeremiah takes, and for
what reasons, in 32:1-16.

_____

_____

> In chapter 32, "Jeremiah's faith in the Lord's words of restoration in chapters 30–31 is now put to the test."[20]

I knew that this was the word of the LORD (32:8). "Everything here reveals the man of faith, not of unconsidered impulse. The outspokenness which had put Jeremiah in custody (32:3-5) is now matched by his humble openness to what God might have in mind to say to him there. . . . Since the early, doubt-ridden days (15:18; 20:7), he has learnt, and still teaches the rest of us, to recognize the hidden hand of God in what befalls him, from whatever human quarter it may arise."[21]

So I bought the field (32:9). "After the Exile the deeds would be of great value to the owners. Here, then, is an instance of ancient title insurance."[22]

8. What are the main points of Jeremiah's prayer in 32:16-25?

_____

_____

_____

_____

Nothing is too hard for you (32:17). "After the bold gesture [in 32:9-12], a daring plea—for Jeremiah is quick to explore the possibility that God might be opening a door of last-minute mercy for Jerusalem. . . . It is a fine example of the way to pray in a desperate situation: concentrating first on the creative power (32:17)

85

Optional Application: How do you see Jeremiah's prayer in 32:16-25 as a model for your own praying? In what current circumstances of your life would a prayer of this kind be particularly appropriate?

For Further Study:
To better understand the "everlasting covenant" mentioned in Jeremiah 32:40, what do you discover in these passages: Psalm 105:8; Isaiah 55:3; 61:8-9; Jeremiah 50:5; Ezekiel 16:60; 37:26-27; Hosea 2:19-20; Luke 1:72; Hebrews 13:20?

and perfect fidelity and justice (verses 18-19) of God; remembering next his great redemptive acts (20-23a; to which the Christian can now add the greatest of them all) — and then with this background, laying before God the guilt of the past (23b), the hard facts of the present (24) and the riddle of the future (25)."[23]

9. In 32:26-35, what are the main points in the Lord's reply to Jeremiah's prayer?

_____

_____

_____

_____

I am the LORD, the God of all mankind. Is anything too hard for me? (32:27). "It was a rhetorical question, a question to which the answer is so obvious that it goes without saying. . . . Asking rhetorical questions seems to be God's favorite strategy for dealing with impertinent prayers."[24]

I will make an everlasting covenant with them (32:40). Recall 31:31-34.

10. Summarize the promises given to God's people in 32:36-44.

_____

_____

_____

11. What is especially emphasized about God's character in chapter 32?

_____

_____

_____

I will bring them back to this place (32:37); I
will bring Judah and Israel back from captivity
(33:7). Recall the promises seen earlier in 25:11-
14 and 29:10.

"This chapter concludes the Book of
Consolation. . . . The theme of chapter 33
is the restoration of Jerusalem and the
reestablishment of its worship."[25]

12. Summarize the promises given to God's people
in 33:1-13.

_____

_____

_____

_____

Call to me and I will answer you and tell you
great and unsearchable things you do not
know (33:3). "In other words, although God
can make himself heard, and has already
done so in saying this, nevertheless to reveal
all that he wants to say, he desires a hearer
who is already reaching out to him. This is
why prayer is never superfluous to the study
of Scripture or the quest for guidance. God
is then speaking to an upturned face, not a
preoccupied back."[26] "The word 'unsearchable' in verse 3 implies that the knowledge of
divine things is inaccessible, incomprehen-
sible, impregnable. Later Jeremiah will use the
same word to describe a fortified city (34:7).
The things of God are out of reach. The things
God has planned to do in the future, especially, are hidden from our sight. The Apostle
Paul asked, 'Who has known the mind of the
Lord?' (Romans 11:34). The answer, of course,
is that no one has ever known the mind of
God. Yet God invited Jeremiah to search the
divine mind. He promised to make known the
unknowable things. He pledged to reveal the

Optional Application: How do you see the words of Jeremiah 33:3 as applying to your own prayer life, your study of the Scriptures, and your seeking of God's guidance in your life?

For Further Study: How do God's instructions in Jeremiah 33:3 compare and connect with what you see in these passages: Psalm 25:14; 50:15; 91:14-16; 145:18; Isaiah 45:3; 48:6; 55:6-7; 65:24; Joel 2:32; Amos 3:7; Luke 11:9-13; Acts 2:21; Romans 10:13; 1 Corinthians 1:2; 2:7-11; Ephesians 3:20; Revelation 2:17?

secrets of redemption. All Jeremiah had to do was call upon the Lord, for 'everyone who asks receives' (Matthew 7:8)."[27]

13. Summarize the promises given to God's people in 33:14-26.

I will make a righteous Branch sprout from David's line (33:15). Recall the similar promise in 23:5. "It is through the Lord Messiah, the righteous One, that the restoration and attendant blessings will be realized. Jeremiah's picture of the coming Messiah, though not so replete as Isaiah's, is nonetheless varied and unique. Jeremiah pictures the coming Messiah as (1) the spring of living waters (2:13); (2) the good Shepherd (23:4; 31:10); (3) the righteous Branch (here and 23:5); (4) the Redeemer (50:34); (5) The Lord Our Righteousness (23:6); (6) David the king (30:9); and (7) the Agent of the new covenant (31:31-34)."[28]

The LORD Our Righteous Savior (33:16). Recall how this same name is proclaimed for the Messiah in 23:6.

14. What's most important for us to see in the messianic prophecy of 33:17-18?

15. What is especially emphasized about God's character in chapter 33?

88

_____

_____

_____

16. What would you select as the key verse or passage in Jeremiah 30–33 — one that best captures or reflects the dynamics of what these chapters are all about?

_____

_____

_____

17. List any lingering questions you have about Jeremiah 30–33.

_____

_____

_____

For Thought and Discussion: Especially from what you see in these chapters, what particular insight has Jeremiah been granted into the character and personality of God?

Optional Application: On the basis of God's truth revealed in Jeremiah 30–33, perhaps the Holy Spirit has helped you sense a new and higher reality in your life that God is inviting you to. If this is true for you, express in your own words the reality that you long for, and use it as a springboard for prayer.

For the Group

You may want to focus your discussion for lesson 7 especially on the following core biblical concepts, which are emphasized throughout Jeremiah.

* sin
* judgment
* repentance
* grace
* salvation

The following numbered questions in lesson 7 may stimulate your best and most helpful discussion: 1, 2, 3, 4, 6, 11, 14, 15, 16, and 17.

And again, remember to look at the "For Thought and Discussion" questions in the margins.

1. Charles L. Feinberg, _Jeremiah_, The Expositor's Bible Commentary, vol. 6 (Grand Rapids, MI: Zondervan, 1986), 558.
2. Derek Kidner, _The Message of Jeremiah_, The Bible Speaks Today (Downers Grove, IL: InterVarsity, 1987), 103.

3. Kidner, 104.
4. Kidner, 104.
5. Feinberg, 564.
6. Kidner, 106.
7. Feinberg, 564.
8. Kidner, 106.
9. Kidner, 106.
10. Feinberg, 569–570.
11. *ESV Study Bible* (Wheaton, IL: Crossway, 2008), on Jeremiah 31:15.
12. Feinberg, 570.
13. Philip Graham Ryken, *Jeremiah and Lamentations: From Sorrow to Hope*, Preaching the Word (Wheaton, IL: Crossway, 2001), 466.
14. Feinberg, 574.
15. Kidner, 110.
16. Feinberg, 574.
17. Feinberg, 575.
18. Kidner, 111.
19. Kidner, 112.
20. Feinberg, 579.
21. Kidner, 112.
22. Feinberg, 583.
23. Kidner, 113.
24. Ryken, 488.
25. Feinberg, 588.
26. Kidner, 114.
27. Ryken, 498.
28. Feinberg, 591.

JEREMIAH 34–38

Under Siege

1. In one sitting if possible, read attentively through all of Jeremiah 34–38, taking notes and underlining or highlighting as you go. What impresses you overall as the key features and themes of this part of the book?

_____

_____

_____

"Chapters 34–38 are largely occupied with Jeremiah's experiences during the siege of Jerusalem. Like other portions of the book, they are not in strict chronological order."[1]

> In chapter 34, "a story about a divinely appointed leader's failure to follow through on his God-given responsibility becomes a story of judgment on a national scale."[2]

While Nebuchadnezzar . . . and all his army . . . were fighting against Jerusalem (34:1). "The time is a little earlier than that of chapters 32–33, since Jeremiah is not yet in prison (Go

For Further Study:
How do you see King
Zedekiah's fate fore-
told in Ezekiel 12:10-
16?

**For Thought and
Discussion:** What
further leadership
lessons do you see in
these chapters?

and speak, 34:2). . . . This was in early or mid-
588, about a year before the fall of the city."[3]

2. Summarize God's message to Judah's King
Zedekiah as given by Jeremiah in 34:1-7.

_____ .

_____

_____

3. What is the situation being addressed in 34:8-
22, and what is the Lord's response to it?

_____

_____

_____

***Those who have violated my covenant . . . I will
treat like the calf they cut in two and then
walked between its pieces*** (34:18). "Here, in
verses 18-19 (see also Genesis 15:9-10,17-18),
we are given our clearest glimpse of the solemn
rite that evidently gave rise to the expression
to 'cut' a covenant (this is the word translated
'made' in verses 8, 13, 15, 18; in the Hebrew
of verse 18 both the covenant and the calf are
'cut'), and of the meaning it conveyed. The car-
cass of the covenant-sacrifice was cut in two,
and the two parts placed opposite one another
so that the parties to the covenant could pass
between them. Whatever else this was taken
to symbolize, verse 18 indicates that it invoked
against a covenant-breaker a like fate to that of
the sacrificial victim."[4]

"Like a flashback, chapters 35–36 inter-
rupt the narrative flow of chapters 32–44
and take the reader back some seventeen
years to the fourth year of Jehoiakim's
reign — a time when the Babylonians

and Syrians had driven many in Judah, the Recabites [or Rechabites] among them, to take refuge in Jerusalem."[5]

4. Describe what happens — and how the Lord uses it as a teaching opportunity — in chapter 35.

_____

_____

_____

_____

"The faithlessness of nearly everyone in Jerusalem (not least King Zedekiah) stands in sharp contrast to the Rechabites, who steadfastly keep their pious vow not to drink any wine as a voluntary sign of their devotion to God. In narrative terms, the Rechabites are a foil to Judah's unfaithfulness and thus serve as an example of the life that is pleasing to God."[6]

5. What does chapter 35 reveal most about the Lord and His character?

_____

_____

_____

For Further Study:
What background perspective can you discover about the Rechabites from the following passages: Numbers 6:2-4; Judges 4:11; 1 Samuel 15:6; 2 Kings 10:15-17; 1 Chronicles 2:55?

_____

During the reign of Jehoiakim (35:1). "Although this chapter returns us to the reign of Jehoiakim (609–589), its placing here makes the sharpest of comments on the promise-breakers of chapter 34."[7]

For Thought and Discussion: In Jeremiah 35, what contrasts can you see between the Rechabites and the rest of God's people?

Optional Application: What lessons in faithfulness from the Rechabites' example in Jeremiah 35 are applicable to your own life, and in what way?

Our forefather Jehonadab (35:6). "Jonadab . . . was the zealot who had joined with Jehu in setting up that king's notorious massacre of Baal-worshipers (2 Kings 10:15-27)."[8]

6. Summarize what happens in 36:1-10.

_____

_____

_____

"This chapter contains a unique description of the writing of a substantial portion of God's Word."[9]

In the fourth year of Jehoiakim (36:1). See also 25:1. This was the crucial year when the Babylonians defeated the Egyptians at the battle of Carchemish.

Perhaps . . . they will turn from their wicked ways; then I will forgive their wickedness and their sin (36:3). "God's statement of intent in verse 3 endorses what he had revealed at the potter's house about the provisional nature of all prophecy (Jeremiah 18:5-12), and it still applies to us. Why else should he pour out threats rather than immediate actions, unless it is to bring us to our senses and to his feet? Why make promises, unless it is to rouse us to the partnership of trust? The issues, then as now, were no less than life and death for a prejudiced and preoccupied generation."[10]

Jeremiah dictated all the words the LORD had spoken to him, Baruch wrote them on the scroll (36:4). "That scroll was destroyed but rewritten [36:27-32], and this collecting of [Jeremiah's] output of the first twenty-three years (see 25:1-3) marks the turning-point in his ministry."[11] Baruch "not only wrote out and read out the scroll of prophecies but almost certainly supplied the narrative framework of the

94

book [of Jeremiah]. What this cost him in toil and fear and in the sacrifice of his bright prospects can be read in the short chapter 45."[12]

7. Summarize what happens in 36:11-26.

_____

_____

_____

_____

The officials (36:14). "A responsive audience, for it was laymen such as these, and perhaps the same men, who had saved Jeremiah from death for his 'Shiloh' sermon not long before (26:1,16)."[13]

Whenever Jehudi had read three or four columns of the scroll, the king cut them off with a scribe's knife and threw them into the firepot (36:23). "It is an extraordinary scene. The king's slow, methodical destruction of the scroll, keeping pace with the steady progress of the reading, made his rejection a far more emphatic gesture than a swift reaction in hot blood. But his further step in ordering the arrest of Baruch and Jeremiah (36:26) revealed the fury and perhaps the fear beneath the show of cool defiance."[14] "Contrast Jehoiakim's utter irreverence for the scroll . . . with the godly response of his father, Josiah, to the reading of the rediscovered Law (see 2 Kings 22:11)."[15]

8. From 36:27-32, describe the responses of the Lord and Jeremiah to the king's actions.

_____

_____

_____

After the king burned the scroll (36:27). "This first recorded attempt to obliterate the word of God is something of a foretaste of the attacks on it in days to come: by skeptics, by persecutors, and, with whatever good intent, by the rash use of the scholar's knife."[16]

As Jeremiah dictated, Baruch wrote on it all the words of the scroll that Jehoiakim king of Judah had burned in the fire (36:32). "Notice that all the words from the first scroll were recorded on the second. Even if Jeremiah had forgotten what he prophesied, the Holy Spirit remembered."[17]

9. What does chapter 36 reveal most about the Lord and His character?

_____

_____

_____

_____

10. Summarize Jeremiah's warnings to Zedekiah as seen in 37:1-10.

_____

_____

_____

King Zedekiah . . . to Jeremiah the prophet with this message (37:3). "This was the second of two very similar approaches to the prophet within a short time (see chapter 21). In the first, the king had asked him to pray for a miraculous raising of the siege, only to receive God's terrifying answer: 'I myself will fight against you' (21:5). Now, however, the siege has been raised, thanks to a military threat from Egypt (37:5), and the king is emboldened to try again for God's favor."[18]

11. Summarize what happens to Jeremiah in 37:11-21.

_____

_____

_____

King Zedekiah then gave orders for Jeremiah to be placed in the courtyard of the guard and given a loaf of bread (37:21). "For whatever reasons in addition to compassion (and Zedekiah's motives will have been as mixed as most of ours), the king did not want the death of this man of God on his hands."[19]

---

12. Summarize what happens to Jeremiah in 38:1-13.

_____

_____

_____

The events in chapter 38 "took place near the end of the siege of Jerusalem. As tensions mounted in Judah, the anti-Babylonian group at court wanted to do away with their chief opponent, Jeremiah."[20] "Jeremiah 38 has many similarities to the story of Easter Week. Jeremiah's experience going in and out of the cistern teaches the believer about Jesus Christ."[21]

The king can do nothing to oppose you (38:5). "The king's capitulation to his princes was perhaps the most abject surrender in biblical history until the moment when Pilate washed his hands before the multitude (Matthew 27:24). The consigning of Jeremiah to the mud pit was intended as a gradual and revolting death (see verse 4); but the king wanted no knowledge of

For Thought and Discussion: From these chapters, what further impressions do you have of Jeremiah's personality and character?

Optional Application: On the basis of God's truth revealed in Jeremiah 34–38, perhaps the Holy Spirit has helped you sense a new and higher reality in your life that God is inviting you to. If this is true for you, express in your own words the reality that you long for, and use it as a springboard for prayer.

it; and the princes, lowering their victim by ropes, took care to let death arrive by natural causes."[22]

Ebed-Melek, a Cushite (38:7). "Ebed-melech the Ethiopian" (ESV). This royal official who rescued Jeremiah from the cistern was of African origin. "Only a foreigner cared enough about Jeremiah to rescue him."[23] His "imaginative care and courage made his act of rescue unforgettable"[24] See the Lord's commendation of him in 39:15-18.

He will starve to death when there is no longer any bread in the city (38:9). "Without his allotted ration at the court of the guard (37:21), Jeremiah was destitute."[25]

13. From 38:14-28, summarize Jeremiah's warning to Zedekiah, and Zedekiah's response.

_____

_____

_____

_____

If you surrender. . . . But if you will not surrender (38:17-18). "To see what hung on the king's yes or no, we have only to read the next chapter for the horror awaiting him and his sons, or to read Lamentations 4 for the living skeletons and cannibals of the city's last days."[26]

Do not let anyone know about this conversation (38:24). "Like a child, he is scared only of having his secret talk found out. His parting words—virtually, 'Don't tell on me!'—show that God's latest and last call to turn back from the brink has not even registered with him."[27] "He feared men more than he feared God (see Proverbs 29:25)."[28]

14. What does chapter 38 reveal most about the Lord and His character?

_____

_____

_____

15. What would you select as the key verse or passage in Jeremiah 34–38 — one that best captures or reflects the dynamics of what these chapters are all about?

_____

_____

_____

16. List any lingering questions you have about Jeremiah 34–38.

_____

_____

_____

For the Group

You may want to focus your discussion for lesson 8 especially on the following core biblical concepts, which are emphasized throughout Jeremiah.

- sin
- judgment
- repentance
- grace
- salvation

The following numbered questions in lesson 8 may stimulate your best and most helpful discussion: 1, 5, 8, 9, 14, 15, and 16.

Look also at the questions in the margins under the heading "For Thought and Discussion."

1. Charles L. Feinberg, *Jeremiah*, The Expositor's Bible Commentary, vol. 6 (Grand Rapids, MI: Zondervan, 1986), 594.
2. Leland Ryken and Philip Graham Ryken, *Literary Study Bible* (Wheaton, IL: Crossway, 2007), on Jeremiah 34.
3. Derek Kidner, *The Message of Jeremiah*, The Bible Speaks Today (Downers Grove, IL: InterVarsity, 1987), 116.
4. Kidner, 117.
5. Feinberg, 599.
6. Ryken and Ryken, *Literary Study Bible*, on Jeremiah 35.
7. Kidner, 118.
8. Kidner, 118.
9. Feinberg, 603.
10. Kidner, 119.
11. Kidner, 29.
12. Kidner, 21.
13. Kidner, 120.
14. Kidner, 121.
15. Feinberg, 608.
16. Kidner, 121.
17. Philip Graham Ryken, *Jeremiah and Lamentations: From Sorrow to Hope*, Preaching the Word (Wheaton, IL: Crossway, 2001), 554.
18. Kidner, 122.
19. Kidner, 123.
20. Feinberg, 614.
21. Ryken, *Jeremiah and Lamentations*, 569.
22. Kidner, 124.
23. Feinberg, 616.
24. Kidner, 21.
25. Kidner, 125.
26. Kidner, 125.
27. Kidner, 126.
28. Feinberg, 618.

JEREMIAH 39–45

Jerusalem's Fall, and Afterward

1. In one sitting if possible, read attentively through all of Jeremiah 39–45, taking notes and underlining or highlighting as you go. What impresses you overall as the key features and themes of this part of the book?

   _____

   _____

   _____

   _____

2. Summarize the fall of Jerusalem as described in 39:1-10.

   _____

   _____

   _____

"The Fall of Jerusalem was so important that Scripture relates it four times — here, in chapter 52, in 2 Kings 25, and in 2 Chronicles 36."[1]

**On the ninth day of the fourth month of Zedeki-
ah's eleventh year, the city wall was broken
through** (39:2). "So the siege lasted for eigh-
teen months, from 10 January 588 to 9 July
587, interrupted briefly by the respite recorded
in 37:5. The breaching of the walls coincided
with the final failure of the food supply, as we
learn from 52:6—which suggests that the
defenses were manned to the last gasp."[2]

**Zedekiah . . . left the city at night . . . and
headed toward the Arabah** (39:4). "Zedekiah,
who has not dared to let God save him and
his city and his family (38:17-19), now deserts
the people he has doomed. His flight, like his
lifelong flight from reality, could have only one
outcome. . . . This was the pattern of all his
choices . . . making him a supreme example of
our Lord's paradox that safety is a fatal goal to
live for (see Luke 9:24; John 12:25). If we would
judge him, we may be judging ourselves, for his
weakness might never have revealed itself had
he not been thrust into a position that was far
beyond him."[3]

"Without doubt, the Fall of Jerusalem
described in this passage dramatically
authenticated Jeremiah's prophecies."[4]

3. What happens to Jeremiah at this time, according to 39:11-14?

_____

_____

_____

**Take him and look after him; don't harm him
but do for him whatever he asks** (39:12).
"From Babylon's point of view, Jeremiah
was a loyalist whose good influence should
be rewarded and given every opportunity to
spread. But behind their action we are to discern the hand of God."[5]

Gedaliah (39:14). "Gedaliah was the son of Ahikam, who had been active in saving Jeremiah's life (see 26:24). For three generations his family had been true to the word of the Lord that came through his prophets."[6]

4. How is God's grace shown to Ebed-melech, according to 39:15-18?

_____

_____

_____

I will save you . . . because you trust in me, declares the LORD (39:18). "The oracle for Ebed-melech [39:15-18] . . . says nothing of the heroism, the compassion or the resource-fulness of his rescue-operation, outstanding though these were: only of the faith in God that was the mainspring of them all. Here, par excellence, was the 'faith which worketh by love' (Galatians 5:6, AV)."[7]

"Chapters 40–44 contain prophecies and a record of events after the Fall of Jerusalem. Chapters 40–42 deal with prophecies and events in Judah; chapters 43–44 with those in Egypt."[8]

5. Summarize the developments narrated in chapter 40.

_____

_____

_____

_____

_____

6. Summarize the developments narrated in chapter 41.

_____

_____

_____

Ishmael . . . was of royal blood (41:1). "Hence his bid for power."[9]

And they went on . . . on their way to Egypt (41:17). "Having been spared the long march north to Babylon three months earlier, and now the eastward march to Ammon (41:10), they instinctively turn south, to gather for a march of their own choosing, into Egypt (41:17). Then on second thoughts they wonder if they should enquire what the Lord might have to say. . . ."[10]

"The narrative continues. . . . At this point the remnant of people were afraid to remain in Judah and were equally afraid to seek safety in a foreign country. Johanan and the remnant were anxious not to make a mistake that would incur the wrath of God, which had already been poured out on Jerusalem and Judah, hence their inquiry of Jeremiah. They did not recognize that by deciding to go to Egypt they had already decided on a certain course of action (see 41:17)."[11]

7. In chapter 42, what do the leaders of the Jewish remnant in Judah ask from Jeremiah, and what message from the Lord do they receive in response?

_____

_____

Please hear our petition and pray to the LORD your God for this entire remnant (42:2). "There were a couple of problems with the Jewish remnant's prayer: The prayer was late, and it was offered by a third party."[12]

Ten days later the word of the LORD came to Jeremiah (42:7). "As once before (28:11-12), we read of Jeremiah waiting patiently for a word from the Lord, rather than producing an immediate and obvious response. Here, at the end of ten days, the reply was anything but obvious, going clean against the fears and hopes of common sense."[13]

I will show you compassion so that he [Nebuchadnezzar] will have compassion on you and restore you to your land (42:12). "The promise . . . puts in a nutshell the true order of things, the order which we forget when we make faithless and prayerless plans. Equally, the natural view of Egypt as a haven (42:14) was one that left out the supernatural view of it: that in the circumstances it was not the place that God had chosen for them. In that event, it would prove (as such havens and objectives do) the very opposite of what it promised."[14]

All who are determined to go to Egypt to settle there will die by the sword, famine and plague (42:17). "Egypt was not in itself forbidden territory; it would become an important center of learning for the later Dispersion, and would shelter the holy family [see Matthew 2:13-15]. The sin of Jeremiah's contemporaries was not geographical; it was a vote of no confidence in God."[15] "Jeremiah was quick to see that his listeners were already determined on a different course of action than the one the Lord had for them."[16]

Optional Application: In the tense and dramatic events in which the refugees leave Judah and flee to Egypt, and in their confrontations with Jeremiah, what do you think are the most important lessons for believers and the church today? What principles regarding God's guidance are especially in view here?

8. From 43:1-7, summarize the reaction of the people to Jeremiah's message to them in chapter 42.

_____

_____

_____

You are lying! The LORD our God has not sent you to say, "You must not go to Egypt to settle there" (43:2). "All along (had they realized it) they had regarded God as a power to enlist, not a lord to obey; and they still cannot believe that his will can be radically different from their own."[17]

---

9. In 43:8-13, what is Jeremiah's further message from the Lord to the Jewish refugees in Egypt?

_____

_____

_____

Take some large stones with you and bury them in clay in the brick pavement at the entrance to Pharaoh's palace (43:9). "Jeremiah performs this elaborate exercise and speaks this devastating oracle. Not only would the carrying and burying of large stones prolong the mysterious prelude to his words, but the combination of act and speech would signify all the greater certainty of the outcome."[18]

I will send for my servant Nebuchadnezzar king of Babylon, and I will set his throne over these stones (43:10). "Nebuchadrezzar invaded Egypt in 568/7, as a fragmentary Babylonian text records. . . . But we have no details of the campaign."[19] "The irony of the situation is unmistakable. Contrary to Jeremiah's explicit word, Johanan and his men forcefully took the

Judean remnant to Egypt, only to learn that Nebuchadnezzar could reach them there and that they would see the very spot where the conqueror would set his throne. . . . Notice how many humanly unpredictable elements Jeremiah included [in 43:10-13]: (1) Nebuchadnezzar's invasion of Egypt, (2) his victory, (3) the very place he would set up his throne, (4) the decoration of his throne, (5) the lives he would destroy, (6) the temples he would demolish, and (7) the gods he would take captive. This passage vividly points out how definite and detailed biblical prophecy can be when God wills it so."[20]

10. What is Jeremiah's further message to the refugees in 44:1-14?

_____

_____

_____

This word came to Jeremiah concerning all the Jews living in Lower Egypt — in Migdol, Tahpanhes and Memphis — and in Upper Egypt (44:1). "This last encounter [in chapter 44] between the prophet and his fellow expatriates evidently took place some months or years after their arrival in Egypt, since they were now settled in places far apart."[21] "This chapter contains Jeremiah's last message. . . . The message reviews the Lord's dealings with Judah and emphatically reminds the Jews in Egypt that their sins have brought on them the wrath of God that had been foretold by Jeremiah."[22]

11. In 44:15-19, how do the people respond to Jeremiah, and what does this reveal about them?

_____

_____

_____

For Further Study: Compare Jeremiah's symbolic act in Jeremiah 43:9-10 with his earlier symbolic acts in the following passages. What patterns do you see? Jeremiah 13:1-14; 16:1-13; 19:1-15; 27:1–28:17; 32:1-15.

For Further Study: In regard to His people's tendency toward idolatry, God declares in Jeremiah 44:4, "I persistently sent to you all my servants the prophets, saying, 'I beg you not to do this abominable thing that I hate!'" (NSRV). What do we learn further about this persistence in: 2 Kings 17:13 and 2 Chronicles 36:15? (Recall also Jeremiah 7:13,25; 25:3-5; 32:33; 35:17.)

107

"This passage is one of the strangest in the book. How stubborn the resistance to Jeremiah's message was! . . . The people openly and unashamedly refused to forsake their idolatry; indeed, they found pragmatic justification for it."[23]

But ever since we stopped burning incense to the Queen of Heaven and pouring out drink offerings to her, we have had nothing and have been perishing by sword and famine (44:18). "This is a most revealing glimpse of spiritual perversity—for in blaming all their troubles on the reformation (44:17-18) instead of on the evils it had tried to root out, these people were turning the truth exactly upside down. Armed with this technique one has an answer—indeed a counter-attack—to everything. Only time would produce its terrible disproof."[24]

---

12. What further word from the Lord does Jeremiah give the refugees in 44:20-30?

_____

_____

_____

_____

I am going to deliver Pharaoh Hophra king of Egypt into the hands of his enemies (44:30). "He would eventually lose first his throne (570 B.C.) and later his life to his relative Ahmose (Amasis), in whose reign Nebuchadrezzar would invade Egypt."[25]

---

13. What does chapter 44 reveal most about the Lord and His character?

_____

_____

_____

14. From all that you've seen so far in the book of
Jeremiah, what would you list as the strengths
of Jeremiah's character?

_____

_____

_____

_____

15. Summarize the Lord's message to Baruch in
chapter 45.

_____

_____

_____

"The message ... was meant to encourage Baruch, who had become disheart-
ened, just as Jeremiah had been."[26]

**This is what the LORD says: I will overthrow
what I have built and uproot what I have
planted** (45:4). "There is a hint in verse 4 of
what it meant to God himself, to be destroying on a vast scale what he had taken care to
build and plant; yet with all this he had time for
this servant (as he had for the Ethiopian Ebed-
melech, 39:15-18), to instruct and reassure and
shepherd him."[27]

**Should you then seek great things for yourself?
Do not seek them** (45:5). In time Baruch
"responded well to the sternness of 45:5 . . . for
the things he sought instead were 'great' in the
sense that mattered, stored up not for himself
but for every reader of what he preserved, from
that day to this."[28]

For Thought and Discussion: From these chapters, what further impressions do you have of Jeremiah's personality and character?

Optional Application: On the basis of God's truth revealed in Jeremiah 39–45, perhaps the Holy Spirit has helped you sense a new and higher reality in your life that God is inviting you to. If this is true for you, express in your own words the reality that you long for, and use it as a springboard for prayer.

Wherever you go I will let you escape with your life (45:5). "Baruch was not to seek great things for himself, but God did a great thing for Baruch. He saved him. As Jesus promised: 'Whoever wants to save their life will lose it, but whoever loses their life for me and for the gospel will save it' (Mark 8:35). The term used in chapter 45 for escaping with one's life is one Jeremiah had used before. God promised Ebed-Melech, the African slave who rescued Jeremiah from the cistern, 'I will save you; you will not fall by the sword but will escape with your life' (39:18). 'Escape with your life' literally is a phrase for taking plunder from a battlefield. God promised that Baruch and Ebed-Melech would escape with their lives as the spoils of battle."[29]

16. What would you select as the key verse or passage in Jeremiah 39–45 — one that best captures or reflects the dynamics of what these chapters are all about?

_____

_____

_____

17. List any lingering questions you have about Jeremiah 39–45.

_____

_____

_____

For the Group

You may want to focus your discussion for lesson 9 especially on the following core biblical concepts, which are emphasized throughout Jeremiah.

- sin
- judgment
- repentance

- grace
- salvation

The following numbered questions in lesson 9 may stimulate your best and most helpful discussion: 1, 11, 13, 14, 15, 16, and 17.

Remember to look also at the "For Thought and Discussion" questions in the margins.

1. Charles L. Feinberg, *Jeremiah*, The Expositor's Bible Commentary, vol. 6 (Grand Rapids, MI: Zondervan, 1986), 622.
2. Derek Kidner, *The Message of Jeremiah*, The Bible Speaks Today (Downers Grove, IL: InterVarsity, 1987), 126.
3. Kidner, 126–127.
4. Feinberg, 620.
5. Kidner, 127–128.
6. Feinberg, 623.
7. Kidner, 128.
8. Feinberg, 624.
9. Kidner, 130.
10. Kidner, 130.
11. Feinberg, 633.
12. Philip Graham Ryken, *Jeremiah and Lamentations: From Sorrow to Hope*, Preaching the Word (Wheaton, IL: Crossway, 2001), 615.
13. Kidner, 131.
14. Kidner, 131.
15. Kidner, 134.
16. Feinberg, 635.
17. Kidner, 131.
18. Kidner, 132.
19. Kidner, 132.
20. Feinberg, 639.
21. Kidner, 132.
22. Feinberg, 640.
23. Feinberg, 642.
24. Kidner, 133.
25. Kidner, 134.
26. Feinberg, 645.
27. Kidner, 135.
28. Kidner, 21.
29. Ryken, 642.

JEREMIAH 46–49

Judgment Against the Nations

The last large section of Jeremiah (chapters 46–51) "is primarily prophetic poetry. The prophetic eye moves from Egypt to Elam-Babylon, depicting in beautiful imagery the judgment of all Israel's enemies."[1]

"Nearly every prophet was given words to speak about the peoples who surrounded ancient Israel — in fact three prophetic books concentrate entirely on a foreign power: Obadiah on Edom, and Jonah and Nahum on Nineveh. If we needed convincing that the God of Israel was seen as Lord of the whole earth, here would be proof enough."[2]

"The prophecies . . . were doubtless given to Jeremiah at different times, though collected here under a common theme: judgment. The prophecies move from west to east. Unlike the prophecies against foreign nations in other books of Old Testament prophets, the nations' sins are not specifically identified; only the judgments are singled out."[3]

For Thought and Discussion: In these chapters, in the Lord's words spoken through Jeremiah to the nations all around, what messages do you see for the nations of the world today?

1. In one sitting if possible, read attentively through all of Jeremiah 46–49, taking notes and underlining or highlighting as you go. What impresses you overall as the key features and themes of this part of the book?

113

For Further Study:
"That day belongs to the Lord, the LORD Almighty," Jeremiah says in 46:10. Explore various prophecies concerning the "day of the LORD" in these passages: Isaiah 13:6-13; Ezekiel 7:10-14; Joel 1:15; 2:1,11,31; 3:14; Amos 5:18-20; 8:9-10; Obadiah 15; Zephaniah 1:7,14; Malachi 4:5.

_____

_____

_____

_____

2. What are the major points in the Lord's message of judgment against Egypt in chapter 46?

_____

_____

_____

_____

The army of Pharaoh Necho king of Egypt, which was defeated at Carchemish on the Euphrates River by Nebuchadnezzar king of Babylon (46:2). "The name Carchemish introduces us to one of the decisive battles of world history, fought in 605 B.C. . . . On the route between Babylon and Egypt, Carchemish (in the north by the river Euphrates, 46:6) made the natural confrontation point; and it was on his way there that Pharaoh Neco had slain King Josiah of Judah in 609 when Josiah tried to turn him back (2 Chronicles 35:20ff.). For the next four years the Egyptian army was based on Carchemish, and Pharaoh dominated Syria and Palestine (see 2 Chronicles 36:1-4; 2 Kings 23:31-35), setting up his puppet-kings while Babylon's main force was preoccupied elsewhere. Then at last the Babylonian army fell upon the Egyptians in 605, routing them utterly."[4]

Later, however, Egypt will be inhabited as in times past (46:26). "At last the horizon brightens for Egypt, as it will for others of these nations (see 48:47; 49:6,39); and we may remember that the prophecy of 12:14-17 goes further still, to offer spiritual blessings as well as material to any who are teachable."[5]

3. What is the significance here of the Lord's message to His own people in 46:27-28 (words repeated from 30:10-11)?

_____

_____

_____

4. What does chapter 46 reveal most about the Lord and His character?

_____

_____

_____

5. What are the major points in the Lord's message of judgment against the Philistines in chapter 47?

_____

_____

_____

6. What does chapter 47 reveal most about the Lord and His character?

_____

_____

_____

7. What are the major points in the Lord's message of judgment against Moab in chapter 48?

_____

_____

_____

"Moab, whose high tableland on the far side of the Dead Sea had formed the eastern skyline for Jeremiah from his

Optional Application: How does the encouragement for God's people in 46:27-28 match the encouragement that He conveys to His people today? And what does that encouragement mean personally to you?

For Further Study: What additional record do you see of God's judgment against Egypt in these passages: Isaiah 19:1-15; Ezekiel 29–32? As for God's "brighter prophecy for Egypt, Isaiah 19:19-25 vies with Psalm 87:4 in the lengths to which it goes."[6]

For Further Study: What additional record do you see of God's judgment against Philistia in these passages: Psalm 108:9; Isaiah 14:28-32; Ezekiel 25:15-17; Joel 3:4-8; Amos 1:6-8; Zephaniah 2:4-7?

For Further Study:
What additional
record do you see
of God's judgment
against Moab in
these passages:
Deuteronomy 23:3-4;
Isaiah 15:1-9; 16:1-14;
Ezekiel 25:8-11; Amos
2:1-3; Zephaniah 2:8-
11?

**Optional
Application:**
Jeremiah 48:10
speaks strongly
against anyone "who
is lax in doing the
LORD's work." Have
there been times or
situations in which
this phrase might
accurately describe
you? What does
God expect from
you in your level of
energy and diligence
in doing His work,
and how does He
help you fulfill that
expectation?

**For Further
Study:** In Jeremiah
48:40 and 49:22,
Nebuchadnezzar is
portrayed as an eagle.
How is the eagle
used symbolically in
other Old Testament
passages? See
Deuteronomy 28:49;
Isaiah 46:11; Ezekiel
17:3-7.

youth, had ties of kinship with Israel, not only through Lot but through Ruth the ancestress of David. It was a bitter enemy as often as not, and its god Chemosh (48:7,13,46) an affront to the Lord; yet its place-names (abundant in this chapter — see especially verses 21-24) were as familiar to Israelites as their own. The thought of aliens trampling its cities and its pastures (48:8) was as grievous to Jeremiah, and to Isaiah before him (see especially Isaiah 15:5-6; 16:9-11; with Jeremiah 48:5,31-36), as to the Lord. But, grievous or not, judgment had to fall."[7]

Chapter 48 in Jeremiah "is the most thorough of all the Old Testament prophecies about Moab. As to its literary values, it has been considered the most polished of Jeremiah's writings."[8]

---

8. What does chapter 48 reveal most about the Lord and His character?

_____

_____

_____

_____

Yet I will restore the fortunes of Moab in days to come (48:47). "There was to be renewal for Moab, as there would also be for Egypt and some others."[9] "The Moabites were conquered by Nebuchadnezzar and disappeared as a nation."[10] "The restoration of Moab is predicted (48:47), but without details. 'Days to come' definitely refers to messianic times."[11]

9. What are the major points in the Lord's message of judgment against Ammon in 49:1-6?

_____

_____

_____

For Further Study:
What additional record do you see of God's judgment against Ammon in these passages: Deuteronomy 23:3-4; Psalm 108:9; Ezekiel 25:1-7; Amos 1:13-15; Zephaniah 2:9-11?

Molek (49:1). More literally, "Milcom" (as in ESV, NKJV). "Better known to us as Molech, he had been worshiped here with rites of child-sacrifice since before the days of Moses."[12]

Why then has Molek taken possession of Gad? (49:1). Gad was one of the tribes of Israel. "Gad was deported by Assyria in 734/3 (2 Kings 15:29, 'Gilead'), leaving its land open to the Ammonites."[13]

10. What are the major points in the Lord's message of judgment against Edom in 49:7-22?

_____

_____

_____

"Edom was evidently well known for two great assets: her wise men and her almost inaccessible strongholds."[14]

His armed men are destroyed, also his allies and neighbors (49:10). "To a people more used to inspiring fear than experiencing it, God speaks of total disaster. . . . So it was to happen. Within a century, the Arabian tribes that overran Moab and Ammon would have driven the Edomites out of their land into the south of Judah; and these invaders would be replaced in turn by the powerful kingdom of the Nabateans."[15]

117

For Further Study:
What parallels do
you see between the
judgment against
Edom in Jeremiah 49
and the one recorded
in the brief book of
the prophet Obadiah?
And what additional
record do you see
of God's judgment
against Edom in
these passages: Psalm
108:9; Isaiah 34:5-15;
Ezekiel 25:12-14; Amos
1:11-12; Malachi 1:2-5?

**For Thought and
Discussion:** Why do
you think so much
space is given in the
writings of the Old
Testament prophets
to statements of
judgment against
other nations?

For Further Study:
What additional
record do you see
of God's judgment
against Damascus
in these passages:
Isaiah 17; Amos 1:3-5;
Zechariah 9:1?

"The severity in all the prophecies about Edom reflects the close and stormy relationship between Esau (progenitor of the Edomites) and his twin, Jacob (progenitor of Israel). Edom's cardinal sin was its pride manifested in its unrelenting and violent hatred of Israel and its rejoicing in her misfortunes (Obadiah 3,10-14). There is no prophecy of future restoration for Edom."[16]

11. What are the major points in the Lord's message of judgment against Damascus in 49:23-27?

_____

_____

_____

12. What are the major points in the Lord's message of judgment against Kedar and Hazor in 49:28-33?

_____

_____

_____

Concerning Kedar and the kingdoms of Hazor, which Nebuchadnezzar king of Babylon attacked (49:28). "Not even the elusive desert-dwellers would be beyond the reach of Nebuchadrezzar when God saw fit to send him. His own motive (49:30) would be doubtless to assert his authority, for these tribes of the eastern desert were a threat to their settled neighbors, who were now part of his empire. (Kedar was an Ishmaelite tribe [see Genesis 25:13,16]; the Hazor . . . either a desert settlement, or . . . possibly a collective term for the unwalled villages of these tribes.)"[17]

A nation at ease, which lives in confidence
(49:31). "As did so many others, Kedar and
Hazor lived in careless self-complacency."[18]

For Further Study:
What additional
record do you see
of God's judgment
against Kedar in
Isaiah 21:13-17?

13. What are the major points in the Lord's message of judgment against Elam in 49:34-39?

_____

_____

_____

_____

Concerning Elam (49:34). "Elam, an ancient kingdom at the head of the Persian Gulf, was the
most distant of the peoples addressed in these
oracles: a trading nation of wealth and, inter-
mittently, of military power."[19]

***See, I will break the bow of Elam, the main-
stay of their might*** (49:35). "As with the
other prophecies here, and indeed with God's
message to mankind, verse 35 singles out
the mainstay of their might for his special
attention. Elam relied on its archers (49:35;
see Isaiah 22:6), Ammon on its Molech (Milcom, 49:3), Edom on its cleverness and its
crags (49:7,16), Damascus on its fame (49:25),
Kedar on its remoteness and its mobility
(49:29,31)."[20]

***I will restore the fortunes of Elam in days to
come*** (49:39). "Grace breaks through for Elam,
as for others. The movements of peoples over
the millennia make their fortunes hard to
trace, but the curtain lifts an inch or two on
the day of Pentecost, when Elamites were found
to be among the multitude who heard of 'the
wonderful works of God' in their own tongue
(Acts 2:9,11)."[21]

14. What does chapter 49 reveal most about the
Lord and His character?

Optional Application: On the basis of God's truth revealed in Jeremiah 46–49, perhaps the Holy Spirit has helped you sense a new and higher reality in your life that God is inviting you to. If this is true for you, express in your own words the reality that you long for, and use it as a springboard for prayer.

15. Compare the messages of judgment against the nations in chapters 46–49 with what we have seen earlier in 9:25-26; 25:15-27,31-33; 27:1-11. What themes and patterns stand out to you?

16. What would you select as the key verse or passage in Jeremiah 46–49 — one that best captures or reflects the dynamics of what these chapters are all about?

17. List any lingering questions you have about Jeremiah 46–49.

For the Group

You may want to focus your discussion for lesson 10 especially on the following core biblical concepts, which are emphasized throughout Jeremiah.

- sin
- judgment
- repentance
- grace
- salvation

The following numbered questions in lesson 10 may stimulate your best and most helpful discussion: 1, 3, 4, 6, 8, 14, 15, 16, and 17.

Remember to look also at the "For Thought and Discussion" questions in the margins.

1. J. I. Packer, Merrill C. Tenney, and William White Jr., eds., *Nelson's Illustrated Encyclopedia of Bible Facts* (Nashville: Thomas Nelson, 1995), 346.
2. Derek Kidner, *The Message of Jeremiah*, The Bible Speaks Today (Downers Grove, IL: InterVarsity, 1987), 137.
3. Charles L. Feinberg, *Jeremiah*, The Expositor's Bible Commentary, vol. 6 (Grand Rapids, MI: Zondervan, 1986), 647.
4. Kidner, 137–138.
5. Kidner, 140.
6. Kidner, 140.
7. Kidner, 142.
8. Feinberg, 656.
9. Kidner, 143.
10. Feinberg, 656.
11. Feinberg, 663.
12. Kidner, 143.
13. Kidner, 143.
14. Kidner, 44.
15. Kidner, 145.
16. Feinberg, 667.
17. Kidner, 146–147.
18. Feinberg, 670.
19. Kidner, 147.
20. Kidner, 147.
21. Kidner, 147–148.

JEREMIAH 50–52

Judgment Against Babylon, and an Epilogue

1. In one sitting if possible, read attentively through all of Jeremiah 50–52, taking notes and underlining or highlighting as you go. What impresses you overall as the key features and themes of this part of the book?

_____

_____

_____

_____

> Chapters 50 and 51 deal with Babylon. They "emphatically stress the truth of Matthew 25:31-46: The criterion by which God judges the nations is their treatment of his chosen people whom he has made the vehicle of salvation (see John 4:22) and placed at the center of the consummation of human history (see Isaiah 2:1-4). . . . Two main emphases run throughout these chapters: the fall of Babylon and the return of the Jewish exiles to their home."[1]

"Fittingly, the empire which struck the most devastating blow ever suffered by the kingdom of David, receives the longest series of oracles about her own future. . . .

"The Babylon condemned in these chapters is the same Babylon whose yoke (said God) was to be accepted until her time should come — and accepted with a good grace (chapters 27–29; especially 27:5-15; 29:7). At the same time, her role as God's unwitting hammer and weapon of war (51:20), as she wantonly pursued her own ends (50:11), would give her no escape from justice. So retribution dominates these oracles; but it awaits God's time and agents. The instruction to 'seek the welfare' of the conquering city (29:7) is not revoked; there is no call to revolution. . . .

"Revelation 17–18 opens our eyes to another dimension of the Babylon of these chapters: as the embodiment of this world's corrupt power and glory, and the archetypal opposite of Zion the city of God. That passage borrows directly from these oracles, speaking of the golden cup with which she makes the nations drunk; of her judgment reaching up to heaven; of her fall, to rise no more; summoning God's people to flee from the midst of her, lest they share her punishment (Jeremiah 51:7 with Revelation 17:2,4; Jeremiah 51:9 with Revelation 18:5; Jeremiah 51:63-64 with Revelation 18:21; Jeremiah 50:8; 51:6

with Revelation 18:4). In this capacity, the Babylon of these visions will have no gentle downfall, but one as catastrophic as anything that the language of ancient warfare can depict."[2]

For Thought and Discussion: What images and connotations does "Babylon" bring to mind?

2. In 50:1-10, what message of hope for God's people is included in this announcement of judgment upon Babylon?

_____

_____

_____

3. What are the major points in God's judgment of Babylon in 50:11-16?

_____

_____

_____

4. In 50:17-20, what message of hope for God's people is included in the announcement of Babylon's judgment, and how does it connect with the promise of the New Covenant in Jeremiah 31:31-34?

_____

_____

_____

_____

Search will be made for Israel's guilt, but there will be none, and for the sins of Judah, but none will be found, for I will forgive the remnant I spare (50:20). "Whether the delightful language of verse 20 expresses what we know as justification, or leaps ahead to our resurrection and sinless state, either way it is our inheritance."[3]

We read in Jeremiah 51:11 that "the LORD will take vengeance, vengeance for his temple." What do you learn about the temple's destruction in Psalm 74:4-7?

5. Summarize the content of God's judgment against Babylon in 50:21-46.

_____

_____

_____

Look! An army is coming from the north. . . .
   They are cruel and without mercy. . . .
   The king of Babylon has heard reports. . . .
   Anguish has gripped him (50:41-43). Recall almost the exact wording of these three verses in 6:22-24, in reference there to Judah rather than Babylon. "The force of this is surely . . . the irony of Babylon's being no longer the menace from the north, but the one menaced now from there."[4]

As God overthrew Sodom and Gomorrah. . . .
   Like a lion coming up from Jordan's thickets (50:40,44). In this prophecy against Babylon, the words of verses 40 and 44-46 in chapter 50 were used earlier in the judgment against Edom (see 49:18-21). "There is little to choose between what awaits the pride of an empire and the pride of a clan—the only difference being in the reverberations of their respective falls (compare that of Edom, 'heard at the Red Sea' ([49:21] with that of Babylon, heard among the nations, 50:46)."[5]

---

6. What are the major points in God's judgment of Babylon in 51:1-14?

_____

_____

_____

7. How does 51:15-19 bring into focus the contrast between the living God and idols?

_____

_____

126

"The irony of the passage [51:15-19] . . . is that originally these words had had to be addressed not to the heathen in their blindness but to Israel in its perversity (see 10:12-16, word for word)."[6]

Optional Application: To the extent that Babylon here in Jeremiah relates to the Babylon in Revelation, what instruction do these chapters offer us in regard to the way we view worldly culture around us, and the overall secular world system?

He who is the Portion of Jacob . . . is the Maker of all things, including the people of his inheritance (51:19). "The Creator and little Israel are everything to one another: the Creator as Israel's portion, and Israel as his inheritance."[7]

---

8. What is the thrust of the Lord's message to Babylon in 51:20-33?

I am against you, you destroying mountain, you who destroy the whole earth. . . . I will stretch out my hand against you . . . and make you a burned-out mountain (51:25). "As a volcano which not only spews out destruction but ends by blowing itself to bits."[8]

These kingdoms: Ararat, Minni and Ashkenaz (51:27). "The three kingdoms of verse 27, all within Armenia, were part of the empire of the Medes (51:28), which spread in a great arc to the north of Babylon's dominions. When Cyrus took over that empire he first extended it westward to the Aegean, to absorb the rich kingdom of King Croesus of Lydia (547/6); then, it seems, eastward to Afghanistan and beyond. In c. 540 he was ready to descend on Babylon after annexing much of its empire."[9]

For Further Study:
Compare the "shout
for joy over Babylon"
in Jeremiah 51:48
with what you see in
Revelation 18:20.

9. What are the major points in God's judgment of
Babylon in 51:34-44?

_____

_____

_____

---

*Like a serpent he has swallowed us. . . . I will
. . . make him spew out what he has swallowed* (51:34,44). "Between these two pictures,
of Israel successively swallowed and disgorged,
there is a riot of word painting, some literal,
and some highly figurative."[10]

---

10. In 51:45-53, what message of hope for God's
people is included in the announcement of
Babylon's judgment?

_____

_____

_____

Babylon must fall (51:49). "That final moment is
decreed here . . . to be echoed in the angel's
proclamation of Revelation 18:2, 'Fallen! Fallen
is Babylon the Great!'"[11]

---

11. Summarize Jeremiah's final message of judgment upon Babylon in 51:54-58.

_____

_____

_____

---

*The peoples exhaust themselves for nothing,
the nations' labor is only fuel for the flames*
(51:58). The wording "is borrowed from

128

Habakkuk 2:13: 'The people's labor is only fuel for the fire, that the nations exhaust themselves for nothing? In Habakkuk, where God is answering the question about the sufferings of the righteous, the saying goes on to add (Habakkuk 2:14): 'For the earth will be filled with the knowledge of the glory of the Lord, as the waters cover the sea.' But Babylon, as the kingdom of man, has no part in that prospect. It has spent itself 'only for fire.'"[12]

For Further Study:
How do Seraiah's actions (commanded from the Lord) in Jeremiah 51:59-64 compare with what you see in Revelation 18:21?

12. How would you summarize the Lord's message to Babylon in chapters 50 and 51?

_____

_____

_____

_____

13. How would you summarize the Lord's message of hope to His people in chapters 50 and 51?

_____

_____

_____

_____

14. What is the significance of Jeremiah's message to Seraiah in 51:59-64?

_____

_____

_____

_____

Seraiah (51:59). "Seraiah, as the brother of Baruch, was a man Jeremiah could trust with a task of some danger."[13]

For Further Study:
Compare Jerusalem's fate as described in Jeremiah 52:12-30 with what you see recorded in these passages: 2 Kings 25:8-21; 2 Chronicles 36:17-21; Ezekiel 5:2-4.

For Thought and Discussion: From what you've seen throughout this book, how would you summarize the particular insight Jeremiah was granted into the character and personality of God?

Optional Application: On the basis of God's truth revealed in the book of Jeremiah, perhaps the Holy Spirit has helped you sense a new and higher reality in your life that God is inviting you to. If this is true for you, express in your own words the reality that you long for, and use it as a springboard for prayer.

15. Summarize the historical events as narrated in chapter 52.

_____

_____

_____

_____

Jeremiah 52 serves as a historical appendix to the book of Jeremiah. "Its tragic record shows the sober truth of Jeremiah's warnings, proving them to be anything but the 'jeremiads' of a pessimist. . . . The closing paragraph, too, bears out his message, which looked beyond captivity to restoration."[14]

"The purpose of the chapter is to show how Jeremiah's prophecies were fulfilled in contrast to those of the false prophets."[15]

Chapter 52 follows closely the wording of 2 Kings 24:18–25:30. The final sentences of the two books (describing the treatment of Jehoiachin, Judah's former king, in Babylonian captivity) are the same. "These verses [52:31-34] conclude Jeremiah's somberly beautiful book with a comforting thought . . . that the Lord did not forget the Davidic line, even in exile."[16]

He spoke kindly to him and gave him a seat of honor higher than those of the other kings who were with him in Babylon (52:32). "The extra honor of pre-eminence, for the king of so small a people, surely pointed to two things: the wisdom of the peaceable attitude that had been commended in the letter to the captives (Jeremiah 29:4-7); and the gracious hand of God in moving the king to show this favor."[17]

---

16. What would you select as the key verse or passage in Jeremiah 50–52—one that best captures or reflects the dynamics of what these chapters are all about?

_____

_____

_____

17. List any lingering questions you have about
Jeremiah 50–52.

_____

_____

_____

_____

Optional Application: Which verses in Jeremiah would be most helpful for you to memorize, so you have them always available in your mind and heart for the Holy Spirit to use?

Reviewing Jeremiah

18. Recall God's reminder in Isaiah 55:10-11 — that
in the same way He sends rain and snow from
the sky to water the earth and nurture life, so
also He sends His words to accomplish specific
purposes. What would you suggest are God's
primary purposes for the message of Jeremiah
in the lives of His people today?

_____

_____

_____

19. Recall the guidelines given for our thought-
life in Philippians 4:8 — "Whatever is true,
whatever is noble, whatever is right, whatever
is pure, whatever is lovely, whatever is admirable — if anything is excellent or praiseworthy —
think about such things." As you reflect on
all you've read in the book of Jeremiah, what
stands out to you as being particularly true, or
noble, or right, or pure, or lovely, or admirable,
or excellent, or praiseworthy — and therefore
well worth thinking more about?

_____

_____

131

_____

_____

20. Since all of Scripture testifies ultimately of Christ, where does Jesus come most in focus for you in this book?

_____

_____

_____

21. In your understanding, what are the strongest ways in which Jeremiah points us to mankind's need for Jesus and for what He accomplished in His death and resurrection?

_____

_____

_____

_____

For the Group

You may want to focus your discussion for lesson 11 especially on the following core biblical concepts, which are emphasized throughout Jeremiah.

- sin
- judgment
- repentance
- grace
- salvation

The following numbered questions in lesson 11 may stimulate your best and most helpful discussion: 1, 12, 13, 15, 16, and 17.

Allow enough discussion time to look back together and review all of Jeremiah as a whole. You can use the numbered questions 18–21 in this lesson to help you do that.

Once more, look also at the questions in the margins under the heading "For Thought and Discussion."

1. Charles L. Feinberg, *Jeremiah*, The Expositor's Bible Commentary, vol. 6 (Grand Rapids, MI: Zondervan, 1986), 672.
2. Derek Kidner, *The Message of Jeremiah*, The Bible Speaks Today (Downers Grove, IL: InterVarsity, 1987), 148–149.
3. Kidner, 150.
4. Kidner, 151.
5. Kidner, 151.
6. Kidner, 152.
7. Kidner, 152.
8. Kidner, 153.
9. Kidner, 153.
10. Kidner, 154.
11. Kidner, 155.
12. Kidner, 156.
13. Kidner, 156.
14. Kidner, 162.
15. Feinberg, 687.
16. Feinberg, 691.
17. Kidner, 162.

THE BOOK OF LAMENTATIONS

A People's Desolation

The book of Lamentations "is closely related to the events described in the book of Jeremiah. It is not so much a sequel to Jeremiah, however, as it is a response."[1]

Lamentations "is not an emotional outburst but a formal expression of grief in a high literary style."[2] "From its opening line to its final question, Lamentations is strongly unified by its almost unrelenting atmosphere of grief."[3]

"Lamentations deals with the problem of national suffering. While there is no effort to minimize Judah's sin, the writer is clearly overwhelmed by the greatness of her doom. . . . Yet there is a clear recognition that the disaster was caused by God, not his enemies. Even the mockery of Judah's enemies was caused by God (2:17). Hence, the laments are shot through with prayer; and prayer leads to hope in a situation in which hope appears meaningless."[4]

This book "is written in a very beautiful poetic style," with each chapter consisting of a poem; "each of the five poems has a distinctive poetic character and a distinctive theme. There is no unifying structure to the book as a whole. Each poem is complete in itself."[5]

"These chapters are built on the basis of an alphabetic acrostic. Chapters 1–2 each contain twenty-two verses, each verse having three lines, and the first word of each verse showing the acrostic letter. Chapter 4 is on the same pattern but has only two lines to a verse. Chapter 3, with sixty-six verses, has three verses for each letter of the alphabet."[6]

135

"It seems that Lamentations has a rhythm all its own. The poetic phrasing used throughout the book is distinctive. Some think the Jews used this special cadence for funerals and other occasions of sorrow."[7]

Who wrote Lamentations? "The vividness of the pictures points clearly to the work of an eyewitness. . . . The impression created by the laments as a whole is that they were composed in or near the ruins of Jerusalem itself."[8] The Septuagint—the ancient Greek translation of the Old Testament which was in common use in Jesus' day—includes an introductory verse to Lamentations that names Jeremiah as the author.[9] However, in the Hebrew text, the book is anonymous. It may be that Jeremiah wrote only part of the book (such as chapter 3).[10] The lack of any mention in Lamentations of the promised national restoration which was central in the book of Jeremiah might seem to weigh against Jeremiah's authorship of Lamentations.

With such considerations, "it is best to treat Lamentations as the book itself does. That means accepting it as (1) an anonymous work that agrees with the theology of books like Deuteronomy and Jeremiah; (2) a literary masterpiece; and (3) a work that reflects eyewitness testimony."[11]

1. In one sitting if possible, read attentively through all of Lamentations, taking notes and underlining or highlighting as you go. What impresses you overall as the key features and themes of this book?

   _____

   _____

   _____

The lament in chapter 1 "is evidently somewhat later than chapters 2, 4, 5 (chapter 3 is undatable). The writer was no longer stunned by the utter brutality of defeat and destruction but was able to see what had happened in perspective. Jerusalem mourned by this time less for what she had suffered than for what she had become."[12]

2. Summarize the sense of desertion, desolation, and shame that you see in Lamentations 1 — and identify the lines there that communicate these things most powerfully.

_____

_____

_____

_____

Once . . . great among the nations! (1:1). "Israel as God's land and Jerusalem as the city of God's sanctuary always held the hope of seeing Yahweh's universal kingship."[13]

Her lovers . . . her friends (1:2). "These terms (see Jeremiah 4:30; 30:14) are best explained by Ezekiel 23 and Hosea 8:9-10. . . . Once the monarchy was firmly established, Israel was always faced with an inescapable choice. She could rely on God for her safety against external aggression, or she could turn to allies great and small."[14]

They barter their treasures for food (1:11). "Theodoret (c. A.D. 450) suggested what is probably the true meaning of the statement — 'They gave their darlings [their children] for food to keep alive.' This use of 'treasures' may be found in Hosea 9:16. It is unimportant whether we think of them eating their children (see 2:20; 4:10) or selling them into slavery. Probably both are intended."[15]

Look, Lord, and consider, for I am despised (1:11). "We are to think of Jerusalem's being so moved by the poet's words that she broke out in a prayer."[16] The sentence is also translated, "Look, O Lord, and see how cheap I am accounted."[17]

The day of his fierce anger (1:12). "'The day of his fierce anger' is the Day of the Lord."[18] Lamentations "is the only book in the Bible written by a person who endured one manifestation of the divine judgment the Bible consistently calls 'the day of the Lord' (see Joel 2:1-2; Amos 5:18; Zephaniah 1:14-16). . . . Lamentations agrees with the emphasis on 'the day of the Lord' found in the prophetic books. This 'day' is the day God comes to judge sin. It can occur in historical contexts like 587 B.C., or it can occur at the end of time and be the final 'day of the Lord.' Regardless, such 'days' do occur, and people need to take seriously the warnings about such days in Lamentations and the rest of the Bible."[19]

From on high he sent fire (1:13). "Not Jerusalem's enemies, but God himself had entrapped the city, bringing it to an inescapable and ignominious end (see Ezekiel 12:13; 17:20)."[20]

The Lord is righteous, yet I rebelled against his command (1:18). "The book of Lamentations is one long illustration of the eternal principle that "a man reaps what he sows" (Galatians 6:7)."[21]

Deal with them as you have dealt with me (1:22). See also 3:64-66. "Jerusalem's one hope is Yahweh's judgment on her enemies, though she did not expect restoration as a result. . . . The very fact that Jerusalem's one hope and comfort (verses 20-21) was the similar fate awaiting her enemies is . . . testimony to the utter shock the Fall of Jerusalem caused even among the godly."[22]

In chapter 2, "the dead still lay on the streets unburied. This would explain why the first lament, though the latest in time, is placed first. Initially the sheer impact of physical disaster is overwhelming; it is only later that the shame of it all is seen as even worse."[23]

3. From Lamentations 2, describe the destruction that is portrayed and the reason for it, and identify the lines where this is communicated most powerfully.

_____

_____

_____

_____

_____

For Further Study:
The last lines of Lamentations 2:15 appear to quote Psalm 48. How does the picture of Jerusalem compare and connect with the picture given in Lamentations?

He has cut off every horn of Israel. He has withdrawn his right hand (2:3). "Both actively and passively, God had destroyed his people."[24]

Like a foe he has slain. . . . The Lord is like an enemy; he has swallowed up Israel. He has swallowed up all her palaces and destroyed her strongholds (2:4-5). "What was amazing about these losses was that they were all the Lord's doing. To be sure, they were the result of Judah's sin. But the reality still had to be faced: God had turned against his own people. He had not simply allowed his own city to be defeated—he had helped destroy it. God had used the Babylonians to do the destroying, of course, but he was still the ultimate cause of Jerusalem's affliction. God had hurled down the temple and torn down the battlements. God had burned the city and left its people to die in the streets."[25]

His dwelling . . . his place of meeting (2:6). The temple.

Her king and her princes are exiled among the nations (2:9). "Surely Jehoiachin is meant, and his ministers in exile."[26]

My eyes fail from weeping, I am in torment within (2:11). "The poet joined in the mourning in language that shows his physical participation."[27]

You walls . . . let your tears flow like a river (2:18). "It is a call for everything, including the ruins, to join in the prayer of anguish."[28]

Optional Application: Reflect deeply on the example given us in Lamentations 3:21-24. What truths of God's love and character do you need to "call to mind" for a greater experience of hope and confidence?

For Further Study: As you reflect on the statement "The LORD is my portion" (Lamentations 3:24), explore what you see of this concept (and the settings for it) in Psalm 16:5; 73:26; 119:57; and 142:5.

Some scholars and Bible teachers believe that in chapter 3, personified Jerusalem or Judah is speaking; others hold that this is more likely the voice of an individual, perhaps Jeremiah.[29] "Chapter 3 presents an individual who counsels Jerusalem to turn to God, just as he has done. His counsel includes statements of what he endured, and of the justice of what he endured, and of the way he came to trust in God's faithfulness."[30]

4. In Lamentations 3, what is the writer's ultimate view of God, and in what lines is this communicated most clearly?

_____

_____

_____

_____

Bitterness (3:5). "The ultimate poverty—the loss of all hope."[31]

Hope (3:21). "The 'hope' that the writer expressed here is not created by denying or minimizing suffering and misery. Rather, these are transformed when the mind is turned to God."[32]

Great love (3:22). "The covenant love and loyalty of the Lord. . . . The covenant had called Israel into existence, and the Lord's loving mercy to what he had created would not end."[33]

New every morning (3:23). "The very fact of awakening to a new day is in itself a renewal of God's mercy. Man has passed safely through the night, a foreshadowing of death."[34]

The LORD is my portion; therefore I will wait for him (3:24). "The poet says, in effect, that he has had so little of this world's goods and pleasures because his share has been the Lord."[35]

Wait quietly for the salvation of the Lord (3:26).
"Here there is the acceptance of God's time and God's will (verse 25), faith expressing itself in quiet hope and the learning of discipline (verse 26)."[36] "This is not the passive waiting of stoic endurance. It is rather an active resting in the goodness of God, with the hopeful expectation that someday one's trials will come to an end. There are times when the only thing a sufferer can do is wait for God. But waiting is good because God is worth waiting for. His salvation will come in due course, provided one surrenders to his will and to his timing."[37]

"In his anguish this poet of the Exile is able to affirm that God is still merciful and faithful (3:22-36). This is the covenant God of Abraham, Isaac, and Jacob, whose faithfulness to the patriarchs was a continuing foundation for new appeals to Israel and Judah to put their trust in Him (Micah 7:20). Lamentations may be counted, perhaps with Abraham himself, as one of the supreme examples in the Old Testament of faith in God. Jeremiah had prophesied that there would be a definite end to the Babylonian exile (Jeremiah 25:11). Lamentations looks for such an end, and even hopes that Judah's enemies will be judged for their crimes against her. In this hope there is an understanding of the sovereignty of God over all the nations, the sovereignty that embraces all mysteries (3:37-39). . . . Lamentations points beyond the humiliation of Jerusalem to the humiliation and exaltation of Christ. With this anchor, the world can know that God is

For Further Study: Lamentations 3:44 speaks of God covering Himself with a cloud. How do you also see this image in the following passages, and what significance do you see for it: Exodus 20:21; 40:34-35; Leviticus 16:2; 1 Kings 8:10,12; Psalm 18:9,11; 97:2; Isaiah 6:4; Nahum 1:3; Matthew 17:5; Acts 1:9?

good, and He will do good in His time 'to those who wait for Him' (3:25)."[38]

Let us lift up our hearts and our hands (3:41). "They lift up not merely their hands, the normal position for petition, but the whole inner man to God; in other words, no mere formal prayer was involved."[39]

My eyes will flow unceasingly, without relief (3:49). "The Bible finds room for every element of human experience, including overwhelming human sorrow. . . . In such a position even the comfortable words of Scripture do not always bring solace and a ray of light. Though Jeremiah had set a limit to Babylonian rule (25:11-12) and had promised national restoration (chapters 30–31), the hearts of the survivors were too stunned to appreciate the promises, of which there is no trace in Lamentations. Even in the era of the gospel, the same thing occasionally happens; then the brokenhearted who turn to these laments discover that they are not the first to pass through thick darkness before emerging into the sunlight again. So they realize that their God is the one who puts their tears onto his scroll (Psalm 56:8)."[40]

"We may reasonably date this lament [chapter 4] not very long after chapter 2. Sufficient time had elapsed for the first shock to wear off, and the poet was able to bring what had happened to a focus, and so supplements chapter 2."[41]

5. What is the essence of the holy city's condition as portrayed in Lamentations 4, and what lines communicate this most strongly?

_____

_____

_____

_____

_____

Her prophets and . . . her priests, who shed within her the blood of the righteous (4:13). "We are here dealing with one of the fundamental concepts of prophetic ethics. Ezekiel 22:1-12 shows that the concept of bloodshed was far wider than murder or homicide; all that cut at the roots of society or that deprived men of their land and livelihood shortened their lives and so was bloodshed. Priest and prophet contributed positively and negatively— positively by advocating or condoning such behavior, negatively by failing to condemn those who wronged their fellow men."[42] "Jerusalem was suffering at the hands of God's justice. But what had aroused his anger? More than anything else, what had invited divine judgment was the negligence of the city's spiritual leaders."[43]

Our pursuers . . . chased us over the mountains and lay in wait for us in the desert (4:19). "It is reasonably likely that the vivid memory of Zedekiah's last, desperate attempt to escape (Jeremiah 52:6-9) lies behind verses 19-20."[44]

In chapter 5, "though there are some references to incidents during the siege, the lament deals mainly with the sequel, which suggests some lapse of time."[45] "Chapter 5 is a community lament that presents Jerusalem crying out to God and casting all her future on him. Chapter 5 is to the community what chapter 3 was for the individual, in that the whole community has come to accept what the individual in chapter 3 advised."[46] "It is a prayer of last desperation, for times when everything else has failed to bring suffering to an end."[47]

Optional Application: How do the words of Lamentations 5:21 reflect the prayer that God is putting on your heart, for yourself and your church?

6. Summarize the picture given in Lamentations 5 of the people's misery, and indicate the lines that communicate this most powerfully.

_____

_____

_____

_____

Remember, Lord (5:1). "Remembrance in the Bible is never a mere recalling. It always involves resultant action; so this is a call to God to act."[48]

We must buy (5:4). "This verse probably refers to the very heavy taxation that had to be paid if the survivors were to live. . . . Second Kings 24:14; 25:12, and Jeremiah 39:10 make it clear that most of those left in Judah were the very poor, who were expected to keep the fields and vineyards in order."[49]

We submitted to Egypt and Assyria (5:6). "Hosea (in Hosea 2:5,8) . . . shows Israel worshiping the Baalim, the fertility gods of nature. This reduced Yahweh for them to a god among gods, and so they sought alliances with Egypt and Assyria (Hosea 5:13; 7:11; 12:1). Now their descendants had reaped the bitter harvest, as Samaria had done a century and a half earlier."[50]

Mount Zion . . . lies desolate, with jackals prowling over it (5:18). "The supreme sign of God's anger was that the temple mount had become the abode of wild animals."[51]

Restore us to yourself, O Lord, that we may return (5:21). "Suddenly there was the overwhelming realization that true repentance is possible only as initiated by an act of God (see Jeremiah 31:18,33-34; Ezekiel 36:26-27). This is a foreshadowing of the New Testament doctrine of regeneration. Unfortunately, it was grasped by few at the time."[52]

Utterly rejected (5:22). "It seems strange to many that one who could so pour out his heart to God should receive so little consolation. There was not even the burning hope of return and restoration that had been voiced by Jeremiah and Ezekiel. The simple fact is that the people of Israel—with few exceptions—had so failed to grasp God's revelation that an experience parallel to the bondage in Egypt and a new Exodus were needed to prepare Israel for the appearance of her Messiah and the world's Savior."[53]

"The book ends the way God intended it to end, with . . . unresolved anguish. . . .

"There are many times when Christians find themselves asking the same kinds of questions: Has God rejected me? Can I still be saved? Is there any hope? Will my sufferings ever come to an end? In this troubled world, similar questions often need to be asked about the sufferings of others: Why does God allow persecution and oppression? What purpose does he hope to accomplish through warfare and famine? . . .

"Lamentations does not have all the answers to the problem of suffering. One thing it does do, however, is raise some of the kinds of questions God has answered in Jesus Christ."[54]

7. Overall, how does the book of Lamentations communicate the deadly destructiveness of sin?

_____

_____

_____

8. Overall, what does Lamentations reveal about the Lord's discipline of His people?

_____

_____

_____

9. How does the book of Lamentations affirm God's sovereignty, even in such a tragedy as Jerusalem's desolation?

_____

_____

_____

"Ultimately there are depths in God's actions that finite man cannot grasp. God's revelation in word and act consistently shows his justice and covenant love; yet there is always a residue of human experience that demands our bowing to a wisdom too high for our understanding. This finds its supreme example in the Cross and in the cry of Jesus in Mark 15:34. This is why every facile theory of the Atonement has failed to satisfy for long, for there are depths concealed in Golgotha that pass human understanding. Only when in glory we see free will and predestination reconciled will we also grasp how God's sovereign will is compatible with his justice and covenant love to his people."[55]

10. What would you select as the key verse or passage in the book of Lamentations — one that best captures or reflects the dynamics of what these chapters are all about?

_____

_____

_____

Optional Application: On the basis of God's truth revealed in the book of Lamentations, perhaps the Holy Spirit has helped you sense a new and higher reality in your life that God is inviting you to. If this is true for you, express in your own words the reality that you long for, and use it as a springboard for prayer.

11. List any lingering questions you have about the book of Lamentations.

_____

_____

_____

12. Since all of Scripture testifies ultimately of Christ, where does Jesus come most in focus for you in the book of Lamentations?

_____

_____

_____

"Lamentations is a book that touches the heart by showing the suffering that comes from falling under the judgment that sin deserves. Although Lamentations does not contain any specifically messianic prophecies, it eloquently anticipates the rejection and derision that Jesus suffered for his people. It also finds an echo in the lament that Jesus offered for the very same city of Jerusalem (and for essentially the same reason) on the eve of his crucifixion (see Matthew 23:37-38)."[56]

13. In your understanding, what are the strongest ways in which Lamentations points us to mankind's need for Jesus and for what He accomplished in His death and resurrection?

_____

**Optional
Application:**
Which verses in
Lamentations would
be most helpful for
you to memorize, so
you have them always
available in your mind
and heart for the Holy
Spirit to use?

14. Recall Paul's reminder that the Old Testament
Scriptures can give us patience and perseverance on one hand, as well as comfort and
encouragement on the other (see Romans 15:4).
In your own life, how do you see both the book
of Jeremiah and the book of Lamentations living up to Paul's description? In what ways do
they help to meet your personal needs for both
perseverance and encouragement?

For the Group

You may want to focus your discussion for lesson 12 especially on the following issues, themes,
and concepts. (These will likely reflect what group
members have learned in their individual study of
Lamentations—though they'll also have made discoveries in other areas as well.)

* confession of sin
* holding on to hope
* total dependence on God's grace
* the nature of pain, sin, and redemption
* God's steadfast love and mercy

The following numbered questions in lesson 12
may stimulate your best and most helpful discussion: 1, 7, 8, 9, 10, 11, 12, 13, and 14.

Once more, look also at the questions in the
margins under the heading "For Thought and
Discussion."

1. Philip Graham Ryken, *Jeremiah and Lamentations:
From Sorrow to Hope*, Preaching the Word (Wheaton, IL:
Crossway, 2001), 737.
2. *ESV Study Bible* (Wheaton, IL: Crossway, 2008), introduction to Lamentations, "Literary Features."
3. Leland Ryken and Philip Graham Ryken, *Literary Study*

148

Bible (Wheaton, IL: Crossway, 2007), introduction to Lamentations, "Unifying Elements."

4. H. L. Ellison, *Lamentations*, The Expositor's Bible Commentary, vol. 6 (Grand Rapids, MI: Zondervan, 1986), 698.
5. J. I. Packer, Merrill C. Tenney, and William White Jr., eds., *Nelson's Illustrated Encyclopedia of Bible Facts* (Nashville: Thomas Nelson, 1995), 371.
6. Ellison, 698.
7. Ryken, *Jeremiah and Lamentations*, 738–739.
8. Ellison, 695–696.
9. Packer, Tenney, and White, 580.
10. See the discussion in Ellison, 696, 716.
11. *ESV Study Bible*, introduction to Lamentations, "Author and Title."
12. Ellison, 702.
13. Ellison, 703.
14. Ellison, 703–704.
15. Ellison, 705.
16. Ellison, 707.
17. *New English Bible* (Oxford: Oxford University Press, 1970), on Lamentations 1:11.
18. Ellison, 707.
19. *ESV Study Bible*, introduction to Lamentations, "Key Themes."
20. Ellison, 707.
21. Ryken, *Jeremiah and Lamentations*, 744.
22. Ellison, 709.
23. Ellison, 710.
24. Ellison, 711.
25. Ryken, *Jeremiah and Lamentations*, 749.
26. Ellison, 712.
27. Ellison, 713.
28. Ellison, 714.
29. See Ellison, 716.
30. *ESV Study Bible*, introduction to Lamentations, "Literary Features."
31. Ellison, 718.
32. Ellison, 720.
33. Ellison, 720.
34. Ellison, 720.
35. Ellison, 720.
36. Ellison, 720.
37. Ryken, *Jeremiah and Lamentations*, 756.
38. *New Geneva Study Bible* (Nashville: Thomas Nelson, 1995), introduction to Lamentations, "Characteristics and Themes."
39. Ellison, 722.
40. Ellison, 697.
41. Ellison, 725.

42. Ellison, 728.
43. Ryken, *Jeremiah and Lamentations*, 761.
44. Ellison, 729.
45. Ellison, 730.
46. *ESV Study Bible*, introduction to Lamentations, "Literary Features."
47. Ryken, *Jeremiah and Lamentations*, 765.
48. Ellison, 730.
49. Ellison, 731.
50. Ellison, 731.
51. Ellison, 732.
52. Ellison, 732–733.
53. Ellison, 733.
54. Ryken, *Jeremiah and Lamentations*, 767, 763.
55. Ellison, 699.
56. Ryken and Ryken, *Literary Study Bible*, introduction to Lamentations.

STUDY AIDS

For further information on the material in this study, consider the following sources. They are available on the Internet (such as at www.christianbook .com and www.amazon.com), or your local Christian bookstore should be able to order any of them if it does not carry them. Most seminary libraries have them, as well as many university and public libraries. If they are out of print, you may be able to find them online.

Commentaries on Jeremiah and Lamentations

Brueggemann, Walter. *To Pluck Up, to Tear Down: A Commentary on the Book of Jeremiah 1–25*. International Theological Commentary series. (Eerdmans, 1988).

Brueggemann, Walter. *To Build, to Plant: A Commentary on Jeremiah 26–52*. International Theological Commentary series. (Eerdmans, 1991).

Clements, R. E. *Jeremiah*. (John Knox, 1988).

Ellison, H. L. *Lamentations*. The Expositor's Bible Commentary, vol. 6. (Zondervan, 1986).

Feinberg, Charles L. *Jeremiah*, The Expositor's Bible Commentary, vol. 6. (Zondervan, 1986).

Gordis, Robert. *Song of Songs and Lamentations: A Study, Modern Translation and Commentary*. (Ktav, 1974).

Harrison, R. K. *Jeremiah and Lamentations: An Introduction and Commentary*, Tyndale Old Testament Commentary series. (InterVarsity, 1973).

Hillers, Delbert R. *Lamentations: A New Translation with Introduction and Commentary*. The Anchor Bible series. (Doubleday, 1992).

Holladay, William L. *Jeremiah: A Commentary on the Book of the Prophet Jeremiah.* 2 vols. (Fortress, 1986, 1989).

Huey Jr., F. B. *Jeremiah, Lamentations.* The New American Commentary series. (Broadman, 1993).

Kidner, Derek. *The Message of Jeremiah.* The Bible Speaks Today. (InterVarsity, 1987).

Lundbom, Jack R. *Jeremiah 1–20: A New Translation with Introduction and Commentary.* The Anchor Bible series. (Doubleday, 1998).

Provan, Iain W. *Lamentations.* The New Century Bible Commentary series. (Eerdmans, 1991).

Renkema, Johan. *Lamentations.* Translated by Brian Doyle. Historical Commentary on the Old Testament series. (Peeters, 1998).

Ryken, Philip Graham. *Jeremiah and Lamentations: From Sorrow to Hope.* Preaching the Word series. (Crossway, 2001).

Thompson, J. A. *The Book of Jeremiah.* New International Commentary on the Old Testament series. (Eerdmans, 1980).

Westermann, Claus. *Lamentations: Issues and Interpretation.* Translated by Charles Muenchow. (Fortress, 1993).

Historical Background Sources and Handbooks

Bible study becomes more meaningful when modern Western readers understand the times and places in which the biblical authors lived. *The IVP Bible Background Commentary: Old Testament,* by John H. Walton, Victor H. Matthews, and Mark Chavalas (InterVarsity, 2000), provides insight into the ancient Near Eastern world, its peoples, customs, and geography to help contemporary readers better understand the context in which the Old Testament Scriptures were written.

A **handbook** of biblical customs can also be useful. Some good ones are the time-proven updated classic, *Halley's Bible Handbook with the New International Version,* by Henry H. Halley (Zondervan, 2007), and the inexpensive paperback *Manners and Customs in the Bible,* by Victor H. Matthews (Hendrickson, 1991).

Concordances, Dictionaries, and Encyclopedias

A **concordance** lists words of the Bible alphabetically along with each verse in which the word appears. It lets you do your own word studies. An *exhaustive* concordance lists every word used in a given translation, while an *abridged* or *complete* concordance omits either some words, some occurrences of the word, or both.

Two of the best exhaustive concordances are *Strong's Exhaustive Concordance* and *The Strongest NIV Exhaustive Concordance*. *Strong's* is available based on the King James Version of the Bible and the New American Standard Bible. *Strong's* has an index by which you can find out which Greek or Hebrew word is used in a given English verse. The NIV concordance does the same thing except it also includes an index for Aramaic words in the original texts from which the NIV was translated. However, neither concordance requires knowledge of the original languages. *Strong's* is available online at www.biblestudytools.com. Both are also available in hard copy.

A **Bible dictionary** or **Bible encyclopedia** alphabetically lists articles about people, places, doctrines, important words, customs, and geography of the Bible.

Holman Illustrated Bible Dictionary, by C. Brand, C. W. Draper, and A. England (B&H, 2003), offers more than seven hundred color photos, illustrations, and charts; sixty full-color maps; and up-to-date archeological findings, along with exhaustive definitions of people, places, things, and events—dealing with every subject in the Bible. It uses a variety of Bible translations and is the only dictionary that includes the HCSB, NIV, KJV, RSV, NRSV, REB, NASB, ESV, and TEV.

The New Unger's Bible Dictionary, Revised and Expanded, by Merrill F. Unger (Moody, 2006), has been a best seller for almost fifty years. Its 6,700-plus entries reflect the most current scholarship, and more than 1.2 million words are supplemented with detailed essays, colorful photography and maps, and dozens of charts and illustrations to enhance your understanding of God's Word. Based on the New American Standard Bible.

The Zondervan Encyclopedia of the Bible, edited by Moisés Silva and Merrill C. Tenney (Zondervan, 2008), is excellent and exhaustive. However, its five 1,000-page volumes are a financial investment, so all but very serious students may prefer to use it at a church, public, college, or seminary library.

Unlike a Bible dictionary in the above sense, *Vine's Complete Expository Dictionary of Old and New Testament Words*, by W. E. Vine, Merrill F. Unger, and William White Jr. (Thomas Nelson, 1996), alphabetically lists major words used in the King James Version and defines each Old Testament Hebrew or New Testament Greek word the KJV translates with that English word. *Vine's* lists verse references where that Hebrew or Greek word appears so that you can do your own cross-references and word studies without knowing the original languages.

The *Brown-Driver-Briggs Hebrew and English Lexicon* by Francis Brown, C. Briggs, and S. R. Driver (Hendrickson, 1996), is probably the most respected and comprehensive Bible lexicon for Old Testament studies. *BDB* gives not only dictionary definitions for each word but relates each word to its Old Testament usage and categorizes its nuances of meaning.

Bible Atlases and Map Books

A **Bible atlas** can be a great aid to understanding what is going on in a book of the Bible and how geography affected events. Here are a few good choices:

The Hammond Atlas of Bible Lands (Langenscheidt, 2007) packs a ton of resources into just sixty-four pages. It includes maps, of course, but also photographs, illustrations, and a comprehensive timeline. It offers an introduction to the unique geography of the Holy Land, including terrain, trade routes, vegetation, and climate information.

The New Moody Atlas of the Bible, by Barry J. Beitzel (Moody, 2009), is scholarly, very evangelical, and full of theological text, indexes, and references. Beitzel shows vividly how God prepared the land of Israel perfectly for the acts of salvation He was going to accomplish in it.

Then and Now Bible Maps Insert (Rose, 2008) is a nifty paperback sized just right to fit inside your Bible cover. Only forty-four pages long, it features clear plastic overlays of modern-day cities and countries so you can see what nation or city now occupies the Bible setting you are reading about. Every major city of the Bible is included.

For Small-Group Leaders

Discipleship Journal's Best Small-Group Ideas, Volumes 1 and 2 (NavPress, 2005). Each volume is packed with 101 of the best hands-on tips and group-building principles from *Discipleship Journal's* "Small Group Letter" and "DJ Plus" as well as articles from the magazine. They will help you inject new passion into the life of your small group.

Donahue, Bill. *Leading Life-Changing Small Groups* (Zondervan, 2002). This comprehensive resource is packed with information, practical tips, and insights that will teach you about small-group philosophy and structure, discipleship, conducting meetings, and more.

McBride, Neal F. *How to Build a Small-Groups Ministry* (NavPress, 1994). This is a time-proven, hands-on workbook for pastors and lay leaders that includes everything you need to know to develop a plan that fits your unique church. Through basic principles, case studies, and worksheets, McBride leads you through twelve logical steps for organizing and administering a small-groups ministry.

McBride, Neal F. *How to Lead Small Groups* (NavPress, 1990). This book covers leadership skills for all kinds of small groups: Bible study, fellowship, task, and support groups. It's filled with step-by-step guidance and practical exercises to help you grasp the critical aspects of small-group leadership and dynamics.

Miller, Tara, and Jenn Peppers. *Finding the Flow: A Guide for Leading Small Groups and Gatherings* (IVP Connect, 2008). *Finding the Flow* offers a fresh take on leading small groups by seeking to develop the leader's small-group facilitation skills.

Bible Study Methods

Discipleship Journal's Best Bible Study Methods (NavPress, 2002). This is a collection of thirty-two creative ways to explore Scripture that will help you enjoy studying God's Word more.

Hendricks, Howard, and William Hendricks. *Living by the Book: The Art and Science of Reading the Bible* (Moody, 2007). *Living by the Book* offers a practical three-step process that will help you master simple yet effective inductive methods of observation, interpretation, and application that will make all the difference in your time with God's Word. A workbook by the same title is also available to go along with the book.

The Navigator Bible Studies Handbook (NavPress, 1994). This resource teaches the underlying principles for doing good inductive Bible study, including instructions on doing question-and-answer studies, verse-analysis studies, chapter-analysis studies, and topical studies.

Warren, Rick. Rick Warren's *Bible Study Methods: Twelve Ways You Can Unlock God's Word* (HarperCollins, 2006). Rick Warren offers simple, step-by-step instructions, guiding you through twelve different approaches to studying the Bible for yourself with the goal of becoming more like Jesus.

Discover What the Bible Really Says

LifeChange by The Navigators

The LifeChange Bible study series can help you grow in Christlikeness through a life-changing encounter with God's Word. Discover what the Bible says—not what someone else thinks it says—and develop the skills and desire to dig even deeper into God's Word. Each study includes study aids and discussion questions.

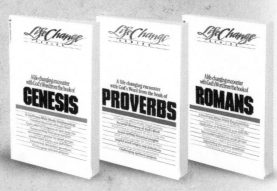

LifeChange $9.99			
Genesis	9780891090694	1 Corinthians	9780891095590
Exodus	9780891092834	2 Corinthians	9780891099512
Joshua	9780891091219	Galatians	9780891095620
Ruth & Esther	9780891090748	Ephesians	9780891090540
1 Samuel	9780891092773	Philippians	9780891090724
1 & 2 Kings	9781615216413	Colossians & Philemon	9780891091196
Job	9781615216239	1 Thessalonians	9780891099321
Psalms	9781615211197	2 Thessalonians	9780891099925
Proverbs	9780891093480	1 Timothy	9780891099536
Isaiah	9780891091110	2 Timothy	9780891099956
Matthew	9780891099963	Titus	9780891099116
Mark	9780891099109	Hebrews	9780891092728
Luke	9780891099307	James	9780891091202
John	9780891092377	1 Peter	9780891090526
Acts	9780891091127	2 Peter & Jude	9780891099949
Romans	9780891090731	1, 2 & 3 John	9780891091141
		Revelation	9780891092735

Over 35 titles available. See a complete listing at NavPress.com.

To order copies, call NavPress at **1-800-366-7788** or log on to **www.NavPress.com**.

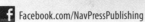